COURAGEOUS CHRISTIAN LEADERSHIP

COURAGEOUS CHRISTIAN LEADERSHIP

Fitzgerald A. Reed, Sr

Carpenter's Son Publishing

Published by Carpenter's Son Publishing, Franklin, Tennessee

Published in association with Larry Carpenter of Christian Book Services, LLC
www.christianbookservices.com

Cover and Interior Design by Suzanne Lawing

Edited by Lapiz Digital Services

Printed in the United States of America

978-1-949572-69-8

Contents

Foreword

"Have I not commanded you? Be strong and courageous" (Jos. 1:9, ESV). These words came at a significant time of transition for the nation of Israel as Joshua took the reins of leadership from Moses. Faced with the realities of leading, no doubt the burden of leadership overwhelmed Joshua. The words of God served as both a comfort and a challenge. While the complexities of leading a massive conquest were pervasive, Joshua's call and task remained sure: to lead God's people.

In an increasingly secularized, pluralistic society in which value systems and traditional social institutions are being questioned and increasingly redefined, the millennia-old call of Christian leadership to carry out the mission of Jesus Christ endures. Whether in the local church, the workplace or the marketplace, Christian leaders are tasked with leading at the forefront of the Kingdom of God. Both the Church and the workplace are faced with ever-aging leadership and a desperate need to develop the next generation of Christian leaders. As the current cultural upheaval causes more and more Christian influencers to question their faith and bow to social pressures, the need for courageous Christian leaders is paramount. Yet, many leaders feel poorly equipped to balance the complexities of modern leadership and the need for developing future leaders.

Courageous Christian Leadership seeks to answer this need by providing biblical principles, practical insights, and effective organizational theories from a Kingdom perspective. Addressing topics such as organizational change, strategic planning, spiritual formation, effective leadership styles, mentorship and coaching, *Courageous Christian Leadership* will educate, empower, and encourage its readers to lead like Jesus: to lead courageously.

-JOSHUA D. HENSON, PH.D.
Adjunct Professor
Regent University Virginia Beach, VA
Lead Pastor
Crossroads Church of Ocala, FL

Introduction

There are many varieties and styles of leadership and innumerable books telling us that one or the other is best. Rather than contending with those various points of view, this book seeks to clearly define a singular and much-needed type of leader for our world: the Courageous Christian Leader.

The Courageous Christian Leader is a born-again believer who follows the spiritual authority of God. God guides this believer by His Spirit to carry out God's Kingdom plan. Rather than wading the aforementioned flood of proposed leadership styles, Courageous Christian Leaders follow Jesus' excellent leadership example. Jesus, as the Servant, transformed His disciples' lives, inspiring them to join His mission. They served as Change Agents who sought to change the world for Christ. Their leadership approach was ethical, transformative, and authentic. They led with a passion for pursuing God's mission at all cost.

This dedicated passion for God's mission on Earth has a long heritage, an example of which is indicated in Jesus' own name. Jesus was known in his native language as Yeshua, or Joshua, an important name for the Hebrew people because of that great leader of their past who led the assault on Jericho. This is fitting as Joshua and Jesus both shared the same passion for following God's spiritual authority. They spent their time and energy serving God's Kingdom. As such, both Jesus and Joshua stand as exemplars for those who wish to be Courageous Christian Leaders. They both carried the mantle of leadership in God's Kingdom and they both passed that mantle to the next generation of leaders.

After Moses' death, Joshua, the military leader of the Israelites, took on the leadership responsibility for Israel. God chose Moses to prepare Joshua, who was the next-generation leader of Israel, to carry the leadership baton. Joshua received God's spiritual authority to lead. He would continue the journey from Egypt to Canaan to lead the Israelites across the Jordan River. But even with God's blessing, like so many of us, Joshua needed encouragement in order to rise to the task of fulfilling his leadership responsibilities. God commanded Joshua to be strong and courageous to lead the people across the Jordan into the land that He promised their father. Joshua had to be a courageous leader in order to follow God's spiritual authority. But he lacked the courage to overcome the challenge to lead God's people. He needed God's wisdom to lead. He needed faith to believe that God would lead him and endurance to complete the task of leadership.

Those tasked with leadership in God's Kingdom may often feel like Joshua—called to courage, but lacking it within themselves. It is hoped that this book can be a source of courage that will help to equip the next generation of leaders with practical steps for leading their organizations, churches, corporations, and institutions by God's spiritual authority. Each chapter provides practical ways to influence organizational cultures in a global context. This book will prepare leaders to lead on purpose, focusing them on the purpose of changing the world for Christ. Then, it will discuss the value of strategic planning and empower leaders toward transformational action. Transformation, of course, begins within, leading to a discussion of the leader's focus on spiritual formation and then to an examination of Jesus' leadership style and his mission to promote the message of God's Kingdom on Earth. Importantly, this includes the need for motivation within the organization. Finally, the Courageous Christian Leader must become a mentor and a coach to the next generation of leaders.

These leadership principles apply across a vast array of organizations as Courageous Christian Leadership is needed across the scope of life. It is hoped that this volume will stir in leaders the courage that is available to them through the Holy Spirit and help them to accomplish the tasks of leadership to which they have been called.

Chapter One

Leading on Purpose

There is a desperate cry for leadership throughout the world. Many professional, civic, and social groups need leadership, but not just any kind of leadership. Leadership can be undertaken anywhere and by anyone. What the world needs are leaders to lead on purpose. Leading on purpose requires leaders to know who they are, what they are doing, and why they serve in the leadership function. This is no small task.

Human history is replete with a debate about the dispositions and qualities that a leader must possess. Is a leader born with certain innate abilities that separate him or her from any other person? Can a leader be developed to carry out a specific task or assignment? Can leadership take place at any time, or during any situation? Many find it difficult to see a single, absolute definition of leadership. Scholars have studied leadership throughout the years, formulating theories and practices to help understand leadership and advance the leadership process.

All of this can make the prospect of leadership daunting, to say the least. But with a determined heart, and a steady hand, the leadership assignment can be achieved. There is hope for the weary and wounded, but there must be intentional actions to gain proven results.

Leadership is more than a concept or an idea; it is a lifestyle that affects every part of one's life. While many have a gut-level grasp of what leadership is, putting a definition to the term has proved to be a challenging endeavor for scholars and practitioners (Northouse 2013). The development of leadership definitions has been affected by world affairs and politics, which have impacted academic studies.

THE EVOLUTION OF LEADERSHIP DEFINITION

Peter Northouse (2013) records the evolution of the definitions of leadership, providing a timeline that illustrates how the term *leadership* has been defined. The list covers definitions from the 1900s through the twenty-first century. The leadership definitions that appeared in the first three decades of the twentieth century emphasized control and centralization of power with a common theme of domination (p. 2). Leaders were encouraged to have the ability to impress their will on their followers in order to induce obedience, respect, loyalty, and cooperation (Moore 1927).

During the 1930s, the leadership concept focused on the traits as defining of leadership, which the idea of leadership as an influence; instead the domination became the emerging focal point. The leader's interaction with a group became identifying traits for quality leadership because the personality of the leader became the primary focus to all other factors, and how other people influenced the leaders. In the 1940s, the group theory approach, which emphasizes the behavior of an individual while leading group activities, was the focus of leadership definitions (Hemphill 1949).

In the 1950s, the leadership definition was dominated by three themes: (a) continuance of group theory, which outlines what leaders do in groups; (b) leadership as a relationship that develops shared goals, which defines leadership as based on the leader's behavior; and (c) effectiveness, which is identified by the leader's ability to influence overall group effectiveness (Northouse 2013). Leadership definitions during the 1960s were predicated upon the leader's ability to influence followers' behavior. Leadership was described as a person's actions that influenced others in a shared direction (Seeman 1960). During the 1970s, the group focus advanced the organizational behavior approach, where leadership became viewed as "initiating and maintaining groups and organizations to accomplish group or organization goals" (Rost 1991: 59). Burns' (1978) definition is the most essential concept of leadership to emerge: "Leadership is the reciprocal process of mobilizing, by persons with certain motives and values, various economic, political, and other resources, in context of competition and conflict, to realize goals independently or mutually held by both leaders and followers" (p. 425).

In the 1980s, the production of scholarly and popular works on the nature of leadership increased. Leadership definitions became a mixture of ideas which involved several constant themes such as (a) doing as the leader wishes, (b) influence, (c) traits, and (d) transformation. Many scholars agree that there is no one standard definition of leadership. Many argue that leadership and management are separated processes, while others emphasize the trait, skill, or relational aspect of leadership. As the world continues to evolve, leadership will always continue to have different meanings for different people because of factors such as growing global influences and generational differences. As Northouse (2013) suggests, "leadership is a complex concept for which a determined definition may long be in flux" (p. 4).

Leadership Is a Process

Perhaps the definition of leadership has remained so in flux because leadership itself is a process. Northouse (2013) suggests four components of a definition of leadership: (a) leadership is a process, (b) leadership involves influence, (c) leadership occurs in a group, and (d) leadership involves a common goal (p. 5). These four components together provide a working definition: leadership is a process whereby an individual influences a group of individuals in order to achieve a common goal.

Leadership Is about Beliefs, Behaviors, and Competencies

Emiliani's (2008) definition of leadership is the "Beliefs, behaviors, and competencies that demonstrate respect for people, motivate people, improve business conditions, minimize or eliminate organizational politics, ensure effective utilization of resources, and eliminate confusion and rework" (p. 34). This leadership definition focuses less on the leader's attributes and more on the effect leaders should have on others in the execution of their day-to-day activities.

Leadership Is Personal

Personal leadership focuses on the specific attributes and skills of a leader. A personal leader is a problem solver, builds and maintains relationships, has job knowledge, maintains effective communication, and implements good work habits (Klagge 1996). They are cooperative, trustworthy, and follow laws and company procedures. Personal leadership is designed to improve the performances of individuals, organizations, and communities.

Leadership Is Shared Responsibility

Today's approaches to organizational leadership focus on transformational, charismatic, visionary, and inspirational leadership as the qualities of top-level leaders (Hunt 1999). Modern leadership definition research emphasizes team structure, participative management, and increasing individual empowerment, where leadership authority is distributed among team members (Edmonstone and Western 2002). The alternative perspective would be shared leadership that enhances the collective and individual capacity of people to accomplish their work role effectively (Yukl 1999). Leadership is viewed as facilitating others' performance (Sarros et al. 2001).

Leadership Is Mobilizing

Leadership is mobilizing resources and people to achieve a common goal. Leadership must be shared among team members, where each member shares in the responsibility of completing the project. Each person must take the initiative to lead in some role or function, which is assigned by the point person, who is ultimately responsible for the outcome. Each team member must be intentional about his or her leadership in order to maximize results. All tasks are essential to the overall scheme of things, so there is no time to waste debating over who is most valuable to the team. All team members are viewed as both leaders and followers.

Leadership Is Serving

A great leader is one who is always searching, listening, and expecting that a better wheel for these times is in the making (Greenleaf 1977). They are always prepared and ready to take the steering wheel of the ship. They may emerge any day, and any one of them may find it their responsibility to lead. Likewise, a Courageous Christian Leader must have a servant's heart that applies the teachings of Jesus. Jesus encouraged His disciples to approach leadership from a different mindset. The secular kingdom rules over those entrusted to them; however, Jesus said, "But not so among you; on the contrary, he who is greatest among you, let him be as the younger, and he who governs as he who serves" (Luke 22:26, NKJV). The great leader is one who naturally has a desire to serve first, instead of seeking a leadership position or title for his or her own ego or to dominate others. Today's leaders must redefine leadership as service and stewardship. Courageous Christian Leadership is purpose-driven, influential, visionary, pragmatic, and ethical.

Leadership Is Purpose-Driven

The world has a desperate need for effective leadership.

Christian leadership must be courageous by being prepared and ready to cross unfamiliar territories. The mission is the identifying agenda of the body of Christ in the twenty-first century and applies faith, commitment, and effective leadership to complete the task. Purpose and leadership go together like a hand in a glove. They both reflect important issues that affect leaders and followers alike in churches, companies, and other organizations. The mission requires leadership to serve and shape it, and leadership involves purpose, focus, and integrity (Lemler 2010).

Leadership must be developed to carry out the mission. Jesus commissioned His disciples, "Go therefore and make disciples of all nations" (Matt. 28:19). He called His leaders to complete His mission. The mission and purpose could not be obscured (Lemler 2010). For contemporary Christian leadership, the same mission remains—spiritual, practical, and theologically inherent. This mission must be the identity and purpose of the church in the twenty-first century, at the forefront of each follower's life and purpose. Serving Christ's mission is and must be the essential function of His body. In this arena, mission effectiveness is most vital and therefore demands leadership that is purpose-driven, committed, and genuine.

An effective leader must have a clear sense of his or her mission at both an organizational and a personal level (Lemler 2010). Strong mission awareness and clarity builds confidence, which is the mark of an effective leader. Confidence here does not mean arrogance or overconfidence; it is indicative of a soul rooted in God and God's strength. Effective Christian leaders will be able to speak clearly and effectively to their surrounding world because they are deeply rooted in an essential understanding of God's purpose. They must endeavor to see things accurately by analyzing God's work in the world and knowing their community's deepest needs. These leaders know themselves because they have done the inner work necessary to understand who they are, what they believe, and how they are motivated. They can see the opportunities that surround them. These active leaders are purpose-driven. They are passionate about their calling and assignment.

Leadership Is Influential

Leaders influence the organizations, communities, and followers they serve by changing the environment. They play an essential role in shaping the futures and career paths of those they lead (Duncan and Walden 1999). Their influence can inspire and equip the people around them to make lasting and significant contributions, not only in the service of organizational and personal development goals, but in the world around them and, most importantly, in the Kingdom of God. Effective leaders challenge their followers by asking probing questions that compel their followers to search for solutions. These questions are strategic, arising as a result of anticipating change and perceiving possibilities. These strategic questions produce a more significant commitment from the followers and cause them to be personally invested in the mission and vision that gives purpose to their work. This is where the leadership baton is carried forward by inspired followers and where leaders must exercise humility and resist the urge to control and micromanage. Leaders catalyze change and allow the followers to control the outcome. Effective leaders provide subordinates with enough authority to perform their jobs successfully, allowing them the freedom to disagree on issues and encouraging them to arrive at their own solutions. Influential leaders know when and where to stretch their team outside of their comfort zone.

Influential leaders are inclusive in their leadership; they allow team members to view, study, and absorb the information at hand and make informed decisions about what actions should be taken. They share their power by sharing information directly and honestly with those they lead and by placing a priority on communicating throughout all levels of the organization (Duncan and Walden 1999). Influential leaders care about the people who follow them. They provide for their followers' personal and professional needs by supporting and caring about each individual's desires and aspirations. They are committed to the people of the organization and understand that the success of the organization, its capacity for change, and its agility in adapting to change are dependent on its people.

Leadership Is Visionary

Visionary leadership foresees the future. Visionary leaders are dreamers, idealists, and thinkers. They envision for today's possibilities that could be certainties for tomorrow. Their beliefs—their values and confidence in their vision and their people—are what will sustain them in the times of difficulty and uncertainty that must necessarily attend this process (Kouzes and Posner 2012). This is especially critical in the area of translating ideas into an inspiring vision. Such translation comes as a result of self-exploration and self-creation, often with no objective logic, but rather a gut-level belief in what must be done.

Visionary leadership, then, is the ability to create and

articulate clear visions and provide meaning and purpose to the work of an organization (Nanus 1992; Sashkin 1992). Visionary leadership inspires others to seek beyond their own self-interest to pursue the group's best interest (Taylor et al. 2014). This helps an organization adapt to its environment by eliminating ineffective patterns of behavior and replacing them with new, more effective ones. Visionary leadership helps the organization to be more effective by providing direction, support, guidance, and assistance.

Visionary leaders must merge their own vision with the larger organizational vision, and then share it with other team members. This communication of vision empowers people of the organization to act (Taylor et al. 2014). People fail to act because the vision is not communicated with clarity; they spend their time trying to figure out what direction to go, which makes them tired and unresponsive (Heath and Heath 2010). Visionary leaders exhibit an attitude and behaviors that influence their followers to develop the necessary knowledge, skills, and abilities to achieve organizational goals (Sashkin 1988; Sashkin and Fulmer 1988). Visionary leadership creates high levels of cohesion, commitment, trust, motivation, and enhanced performance (Zhu et al. 2005; Taylor et al. 2014).

Leadership Is Pragmatic

Pragmatic leaders actively search for solutions to whatever problems arise (Mumford and Van Doorn 2001). Pragmatic leaders assist team members by defining practical steps to achieve organizational goals. They direct their team toward practical consequences or real effects as vital components of both meaning and truth (Wicks and Freeman 1998; Flyvbjerg 2001). Pragmatic leaders reject the idea that truth connects to some nonexperienced or preconstituted reality (Ruwhiu and Cone 2013). Instead, the pragmatist view contends that truth corresponds to the human experience. A pragmatic perspective changes the focus from an individual to a processual dynamic, bringing to the forefront an emphasis on contextualized connections and interdependencies that inform leadership practice. Pragmatic leaders seek practical methods to solve human problems (Mumford and Van Doorn 2001).

Pragmatic leaders understand the importance of acquiring knowledge in order to help others solve problems. Furthermore, they understand the importance of wisdom, which is the knowledge that comes from illustrative practices (Ruwhiu and Cone 2010; Zhang et al. 2011). Leadership is a process whereby leadership and the framework that is practiced are mutually constitutive (Knights and O'Leary 2006). Pragmatic leaders' knowledge enables them to flexibly adapt the most suitable behavior in any situation, because there is a direct connection between the leaders' pursuit of self-realization and the realization of an obligation to respond to the social situation in which they are placed (Ames 2003). Pragmatic leaders seek to add value to a culture that is practical, realistic, and vital. Many businesses today realize that making money and doing good in society are mutually important (Kaugman 2009). Pragmatic leaders commit to adding value daily to themselves, their family, and their organization.

Leadership Is Ethical

Leaders must be conscious of the moral example they establish for their team members, exercising strong ethics in both their personal and professional life. Leadership ethics has emerged as a new and growing field of applied ethics. The study of leadership ethics consists of examining questions that regard right, wrong, good, evil, virtue, duty, obligation, rights, justice, fairness, and responsibility in human relationships with each other and other living things. Ciulla (2014) uses the term "leadership ethics" to refer to the study of ethical issues related to leaders, followers, and leadership (p. 4).

The power of leadership exists in the context of the value-laden relationship between leaders and followers who intend real changes that reflect their mutual purposes and goals (Ciulla 2014). Peters and Waterman (1982) note that the real role of leadership is to manage the values of an organization (p. 245). Values are the ideas and beliefs that influences and direct choices and actions. All leadership is value-laden. That is to say that all leadership, whether good or bad, is moral leadership. Followers expect leaders to consider their rights and needs. Conversely, leaders must recognize the correct roles for each of their followers so that they may make their best contribution to the organization. Perhaps the most important thing followers need leadership to establish in this regard is an organizational values system. Leaders must create corporate values in order to determine what should be done.

Leadership is responsible for teaching followers how to achieve organizational goals fostering learning, and building community and consensus among followers. The task of leaders is to empower the followers with information, offering insight, new knowledge, and alternative perspectives on reality (Ciulla 2014). Leaders must foster moral behavior from the top of the organization to the bottom because, without moral leadership, the standard of ethics will never emerge within the organization. Moral leadership is difficult to define, but it is recognized when we see it. Effective leadership depends on the leaders' attributes and behaviors that fit the strategic organizational possibilities and the leaders who are accepted by their followers (Hollander 2009). Ethical leadership is essential to the leadership process; it helps to build the organizational community and consensus among leaders and followers.

CONCLUSION

While leadership has many definitions, none of which is universal (Lord et al. 2001), we can assert that it is a relational process that goes beyond the heroic model, which focuses on the adoration of a few gifted people at the top of an organization (Metcalfe and Metcalfe 2007). Attention is placed on the senior leadership of an organization because of the power and resources these individuals must effectively implement organizational transformation (Conger 1999).

Leadership definitions have evolved over the decades. Many debate whether leaders are born with specific attributes or are primarily developed through the cultivation of individual skills. Leadership can take place anywhere and anytime with individuals who are willing to work together. Leadership is a process whereby an individual influences a group of individuals to achieve a common goal (Northouse 2013). The leadership process involves the leader and the followers, who decide to join forces to achieve organizational goals. It is not for the weak at heart because the relationship between the leaders and the followers can be challenging if communication, roles, and expectations are not clarified. Organizations are faced with many challenges that hinder their organizational vision and strategies for success. Leading on purpose requires leaders to be purpose-driven, influential, visionary, pragmatic, and ethical. Leaders must be courageous to lead the organization into the future.

Chapter Two

Changing the World for Christ

The world is in a desperate need of Courageous Christian Leadership. Courageous Christian Leaders are the Change Agents who follow God's spiritual authority to change the world for Christ, despite the fear and intimidation; they prepare themselves to move their organizations into the future. That future is frequently threatened by humanity's own inhumanity. Many social threats have existed over the last twenty years, and many organizations are searching for answers, though, often, the deepest, most pervasive problems are ignored.

While governments have been obsessed with the threat of weapons of mass destruction in Iraq, they have allowed the real weapons of mass destruction—injustice and impunity, poverty, racism and discrimination, the uncontrolled trade in small arms, violence against women, and abuse of children—to go unaddressed. (Amnesty International 2004)

The world needs leadership that understands societal problems and engages with other cultures to resolve conflicts and indifference. Regardless of where you live on Earth, you will interact with people with a different culture (Williams 2017). Christ has commissioned His disciples to go into the world to share His message of redemption (Matt. 28:19–20). Christ's message of love, grace, forgiveness, hope, and a new beginning is what the world needs more than anything else.

Courageous Christian Leaders are active in learning about other cultures, so they can guide their organizations into unknown territories, which requires them to be a Culture Change Agent. When most people think about culture, their first thoughts involve race or ethnicity, but culture goes beyond that. People are members of various cultural groups, and cultural identities develop based on the influence of the various intersections of these memberships. Cultures are dynamic and complex, and cultural identity is an ongoing developmental process.

CULTURE CHANGE AGENT

Joshua was the assistant to the Prophet Moses of the Israelites (Deut. 34:5). After the death of Moses in the land of Moab, the children of Israel mourned for him in the plains of Moab for thirty days (Deut. 34:8). Now, Joshua was a man full of the spirit of wisdom; for Moses had laid his hands on him (Deut. 34:9). God spoke to Joshua about moving the Israelites out of the land of Moab and into the land of Canaan, which he promised to give to Abram and his descendants (Gen. 12:1).

God called Joshua to change the location and the lives of the Israelites. The Israelites were in bondage to the Egyptians for 430 years (Ex. 12:40). God, with a mighty hand, delivered the Israelites through the leadership of Moses (Ex. 14:30), who led the Israelites into the wilderness to worship God (Ex. 3:18). The Israelites wandered in the desert for forty years because they refused to trust God. Therefore, God promised that generation would not enter the Promised Land because of their whining, complaining, and doubting (Num. 14:27–30). When that generation of Israelites died in the wilderness, God commanded Joshua, "Go over this Jordan, you and all these people to the land which I am giving them—the children of Israel" (Josh. 1:2). He added,

Remember, I commanded you to be strong and brave. Don't be afraid, because the Lord your God will be with you wherever you go. So, Joshua gave orders to the leaders of the people: Go through the camp and tell the people, "Get some food ready. Three days from now we will go across the Jordan River and take the land that the Lord our God is giving us." (Josh. 1:9–11, ESV)

God gave Joshua the spiritual authority to lead the Israelites into the territory of Canaan, the Promised Land. God encouraged Joshua to "Be strong and of good courage, for to these people you shall divide as an inheritance the land which I swore to their fathers to give them" (Josh. 1:6). Joshua was encouraged by God to "Only be strong and very courageous that you may observe to do according to all the law which Moses My servant commanded you" (Josh. 1:7). Joshua followed the instructions of God and commanded the Israelite officers to prepare them for a transition into the Promised Land, a land flowing with milk and honey. Moreover, the Israelites decided to follow Joshua's leadership as they had followed Moses (Josh. 1:16–17).

Joshua was given the task of changing the culture of the Israelites. They had already moved from bondage in Egypt to the wilderness; next, God was ready to lead them into the land flowing with milk and honey. Joshua is, therefore, a powerful example of a Change Agent. A Change Agent is a person who serves and catalyzes to bring about organizational change (Manuele 2015). A Change Agent assesses the present, is dissatisfied with the organization's current state, contemplates a better future, and acts to achieve the culture changes necessary to attain the desired future. Change Agent leadership must identify future trends and needs, lead change agendas, invest in what makes a difference, and remain authentic and courageous (Baer et al. 2015).

Change Agents Move the Organization into the Future

Change Agent leaders create the capacity and environment necessary to move the organization into the future, while maintaining and preserving the values and core missions that make the organization strong (Baer et al. 2015). Change Agent leaders determine organizations' futures by evaluating their pasts in order to know what will make the organizations strong in the future. Change Agent leaders must assess the value they provide to their followers, communities, and society in order to survive in an ever-changing environment. Leaders must have a courageous attitude and mind-set necessary to move organizations into the future. Leadership can positively or negatively influence organizational culture—that is, an organization's entrenched attitudes and shared values, beliefs, assumptions, and norms that may govern corporate decision making (Manuele 2015). Culture reflects attitudes, beliefs, perceptions, and values that team members at all levels share within the organization.

Change Agents Manage Change

The leader must have the capacity to manage change. A Change Agent is skilled, experienced, and confident to lead the change process (Stonehouse 2013). The Change Agent must be driven and committed to bringing change to successful completion (Stonehouse 2011). Resistance to change should be expected because change disrupts the homeostasis or balance of the group (Marquis and Houston 2009). Leaders must have a positive attitude and reaction to resistance to change; they must be supportive and act constructively toward any opposition (Stonehouse 2013).

Newton (2009) suggests that "resistance is not simply a force to overcome; it indicates a different viewpoint that should be listened to and explored" (p. 257). The Change Agent involves all team members in the process of change and communicates with them honestly and transparently in order to foster trust, develop shared ownership, and gain their support for change (Stonehouse 2012). During the change process, the leader must stay focused on the vital role of managing the organization. The role of the Change Agent is that of oversight, rather than direct involvement (Stonehouse 2013). The Change Agent must accept support from other team members and provide support for staff who are going through the proposed change.

Change Agents Use Cultural Agility

Change Agents must have cultural agility. Caligiuri (2012) defines cultural agility as a practice, not an achievement, and stresses that building it is a process, not an event (p. 5). Cultural agility professionals can accurately read the cross-cultural or multicultural situation; assess differences in behaviors, attitudes, and values; and respond successfully within the cross-cultural context. Change Agents apply cultural adaptation, cultural minimization, and cultural integration in order to change the culture. Cultural adaptation is the process of adapting one's behavior to the norm of a cultural context. Cultural minimization, in contrast to cultural adaptation, is used to supersede the cultural expectations of others. Cultural integration is used when finding that a compromise is most important and well worth the effort.

Global Leaders' performance depends on their ability to function in the cross-cultural context of their task as they frequently work with many people from different countries (Caligiuri 2012). Local leaders must use cultural agility within their home country in order to influence others to achieve organizational goals. Regardless of their context, Change Agents can succeed within an unfamiliar set of cultural norms or multiple sets of cultural norms. They evaluate cultural shifts and adjust in order to lead the organization toward future success.

Change Agents must, therefore, have cross-cultural competencies and cultural agility in order to facilitate their effectiveness in cross-cultural environments. They must manage their responses in order to quickly, comfortably, and effectively work in different cultures and with people from different cultures (Caligiuri 2012). They make appropriate decisions by accurately reading and responding to the cultural context within which they find themselves, while accounting for business strategy and other essential elements, such as laws and regulations.

FUTURE SMART

Courageous Christian Leaders have an innovative mind-set that focuses on their organization's current strengths, as well as its future opportunities and threats. Canton (2015) notes that being Future Ready is preparing, adapting, and learning for the future, and that this leads to being Future Smart, the end state of readiness (p. 1). Therefore, the leader must be Future Smart in order to prepare the organization to move into the next stage of its development. The Christian leader must act on Jesus' words to "Go and make disciples of all the nations" (Matthew 28:19), a task which naturally requires creativity and innovation.

Leadership Pays Attention to Trends

Courageous Christian Leaders must look at trends that impact the world for the next thirty years in order to transform business, markets, society, culture, and the future. They must look at trends in order to predict the opportunities and threats that will affect their organizations (Canton 2015). Trends are hidden forces that shape the future; they are what shape our lives, work, entertainment, competition, and health. Trends are change drivers and reality shapers that emerge invisibly. Trends are joining forces that create market, product, lifestyle, or culture. Therefore, individuals and organizations who can understand and predict trend patterns can start a revolution.

The world as we know it is changing every day. Fundamental changes in technology, population, energy, climate, globalization, and work are emerging, creating a new era, in which acceleration and complex patterns are constantly transforming our world (Canton 2015). Being Future Smart is about looking at the critical driving forces, changes, power shifts, and a shifting landscape, which every person, business, and government must understand in order to thrive over the next thirty years. Future Smart leaders must realize the new intersection of global power, real-time business, globalized markets, disruptive innovation, social change, population dynamics, massive prosperity, and collaboration. A Future Smart perspective informs, changes, and offers scenarios and stories that will affect everyone throughout the world, in every nation, and every city for the next hundred years.

Being Future Smart is a learning process, which includes becoming aware of trends and taking action to shape our future (Canton 2015). Being predictive and adaptive for the future will empower Courageous Christian Leaders to become Future Smart. Future Smart skills require the leader to pay attention to emerging trends, attracting collaborations, redesigning work processes, and rethinking the purpose of organizations. Being Future Smart means embracing radical innovation, being a fast learner, catalyzing change, making bold discoveries, experimenting daily, and collaborating more deeply with colleagues.

COURAGEOUS CHRISTIAN LEADERSHIP AND THE CHURCH

While many may be threatened and even frightened by changes in church culture, the truth is that the church has always been evolving. The First-Century Church, also called Church 1.0 (Cole 2010), was comprised of the churches of Jerusalem, Antioch, Galatia, Corinth, and Ephesus and was kept organic and straightforward under oppression and persecution from ten Roman emperors. The Church established bishops, and Christianity was institutionalized during this period; also, false doctrine emerged and was purged from within the Church. The Church, for the most part, remained a grassroots and marginalized movement under the intense heat of persecution (Cole 2010).

After AD 313, significant changes took place when Constantine became the first Christian emperor of Rome. He declared that the empire would not only tolerate Christianity but would restore to the Church all lost property (Cole 2010). In AD 324, Constantine reminded the lawmakers of the exclusive claims of the Christian God to worship and decreed the suppression of polytheism and destruction of its meeting place (MacMullen 2014). The gathering of Christian believers in private homes continued to be the norm until the early decades of the fourth century, when Constantine began erecting the first Christian basilicas (Lockwood 2009). Christianity became the State's religion and didn't change until the next shift, in which the Church is called Church 2.0 (Cole 2010). In the Church 2.0 era, many changes took place within the Church, but none had a systemic change impact. The Church reflects the body of the Lordship of Christ and serves as a witness to His Word (Van Wyk 2017). The mission of the Reformed tradition of the Church is traced in the biblical narratives in the Word. Such events as the wars, periods of unrest, and instances of corruption in the history of the Church spearheaded the early Reformation process. Both the Roman Catholic Church and the Eastern Orthodox Church were established during this period, but with few systemic changes (Cole 2010). The Reformation divided the Western Church into the Roman Church and the volatile Protestant Church. Whether Pentecostal or Reformed, the church continued in the upgraded 2.0 level; from Baptist to Brethren, from Methodist to Mennonite, the change in the systems were relatively untouched over centuries. Ecclesiological denominations emerged from the early Reformation days, including the Roman Catholic ecclesiology, the Lutheran ecclesiology and the Ecumenical ecclesiology (Pettegree and Hall 2004; Holdcroft 2006; Okholm 2009).

The shift to Church 3.0 is already taking place. Cole (2010) believes the second major shift is occurring now (p. 8). Many think the Church needs to go back to the first-century model, while also learning from the Church's two thousand years of mistakes, and using today's technological advances. With this model, the church could potentially have a significant impact and cause the rapid spread of the gospel. As far back as 1995, Rick Warren called for a new Reformation, encouraging churches to take action to accelerate the transformation process. The Church, in both creed and deed, must reflect God's Kingdom effectively among the lost (Warren 1995). Leaders must, therefore, influence the Church to move from a centralized, institutional model to a decentralized, organic movement, in which followers are empowered to share the gospel throughout the world. The Church must influence society by using Jesus' message to transform communities (Cole 2005). The Church must be active and alive within the sphere of its influence, allowing the gospel to transform people and organizations. Courageous Christian Leaders prepare God's people for the work of serving others and making the Church stronger (Eph. 4:11–12).

Courageous Christian Leadership as a Problem Solver

One place that has already seen a rapid transformation in religious life over the last 150 years is Africa (Manglos 2011). Christian and Muslim affiliations have become universal because of the complex processes of missionization (Robert 2000; Anderson 2001; Isichei 2004; Meyer 2004; Robbins 2004; Jenkins 2006). Protestant Christian, Evangelical, and independent religious institutions are the fastest-growing groups in Africa (Robert 2000; Englund 2003). "Although past research portrays the missionization of Africa as a top-down process, most historians today agree that the spread of these world religions in Africa has been marked by adaptation, acculturation, and integration with pre-existing modes of spirituality" (Chidester 1996; Magesa 2004).

Courageous Christian Leadership Uses Social Intelligence

Courageous Christian Leadership requires leaders to solve problems. It is inevitable that problems will arise inside or outside the organization. Leaders must, therefore, be aware of problems and equipped to resolve issues. This requires leaders to cultivate social intelligence—that is, one's ability to understand the thinking, feelings, and behaviors of other people and to interact with them effectively in various contexts (Thorndike 1920; Kihlstrom and Cantor 2000; Sternberg 2002). This includes speaking in a clear and convincing manner; knowing what to say, when to say it, and how to say it; and building and maintaining positive relationships with others. Social intelligence consists of four types of abilities: situational awareness, situational response, cognitive empathy, and social skills.

Social awareness and situational response are the primary abilities essential for a leader's success (Rahim et al. 2018). Social awareness refers to one's ability to collect information for the diagnosis and formulation of problems, and situational response refers to one's ability to use this information to make effective decisions in order to obtain desired results. Secondary abilities required for social intelligence are cognitive empathy (the ability to understand the feelings and needs of people) and social skills (the ability to communicate with people effectively and to build and maintain relationships). These two abilities can help leaders to remain aware of various social situational contexts in order to improve their situational response competence. Courageous Christian Leadership uses social intelligence to resolve problems in multiple settings.

Courageous Christian Leaders Use Adaptive Leadership

The world is continually changing. One can either benefit from the change or miss the opportunities that changes bring. Denying change is simply not an option. Therefore, change is certain to be a part of organizational life (Hatch 2013). Organizations are increasingly functioning in unpredictable environments, marked by constant changes (Cullen et al. 2013; Wainaina et al. 2014). As a result, leaders will have to be continuous, adaptive learners in order to survive and thrive in the global environment (Schein 2010). Most of the changes being experienced are due to increased globalization, rapid technological change, and competition, as well as changes in cultural values, social responsibilities, and environmental impacts (Muluneh and Gedifew 2018). These changes necessitate adaptation and innovation (Sporn 2001; Yukl and Mahsud 2010). Therefore, leadership must prepare for social and global changes.

Courageous Christian Leaders adapt to the changing environment. Adaptive work includes addressing problems outside of the standard organizational procedures, identifying adaptive challenges, delegating responsibility regardless of positions, building changes on the past, preserving important assets, and progress for the future (Heifetz et al. 2009; Creyton 2014). Also, adaptive work includes learning, encouraging independent judgment, and developing leadership capacity. Leadership capacity includes tackling problems that affect organizational progress. Adaptive changes require adaptive work. Adaptive leadership displaces, reregulates, and rearranges old structures and cultural practices (Sporn 2001). Finding solutions to address adaptive problems calls for a courageous leadership that will not exert authority over followers but that instead will build a willing framework by asking tough questions, challenging the status quo, confronting reality, drawing out issues, challenging current procedures, and transferring the responsibility of solving problems to people who must make the change.

The world is rapidly changing, but does the world reflect

God's image? God desires the world to conform to the image of Christ. He expects the world to operate as the Kingdom of Heaven operates, where everyone and everything is submitting to His spiritual authority (Matt. 6:1–10). The world needs Courageous Christian Leadership to inspire and motivate individuals and organizations to change the world for Christ. Globalization has impacted our world forever, with rapid changes in technology, transportation, and communication, creating a desperate need for leadership with a capacity to be Future Smart, solutions-focused, socially intelligent, and adaptive to change and challenges in order to influence society and culture.

These qualities and skills help Courageous Christian Leaders move organizations into the future. Leader's abilities to learn from trends help identify organizational opportunities or threats, and their understanding of trends in the global environment positions the organization within the marketplace in such a way as to gain success. By applying social intelligence, they remain keenly aware of the needs of others and show empathy, which helps them create more comprehensive and sensitive solutions. This, in turn, allows them to accomplish their mission, both of fulfilling organizational purposes and of supporting others in order to help them reach their goals. Adaptive leadership makes the adjustments needed by regularly evaluating the organization's vision, mission, and strategy, and by developing collaborative developmental plans that improve working performances. Importantly, Courageous Christian Leaders adapt to the environment without compromising their Christian values. In fact, it is their Christian values of love and compassion for others that lead them to be sensitive to changing needs.

Chapter Three

Planning for the Future

Joshua communicated God's strategic plan for the Israelites to cross the Jordan, into the area which was known as the Promised Land, a land flowing with milk and honey. God promised this land to Abram, but Abram had to move into unknown territory (Gen. 12:1). The Promised Land was populated by the enemies of Israelites—the Canaanites, Hittites, Hivites, Perizzites, Girgashites, Amorites, and Jebusites (Josh. 3:11). God used Joshua to lead the Israelites to accomplish the goal of reclaiming the land. God communicated to Joshua, "Be strong and courageous because you will lead these people to inherit the land, I swore to their ancestors to give them" (Josh. 1:6, NIV). God gave Joshua commands to "be careful to obey all the laws of my servant Moses so that the Israelites can have success" (Josh. 1:7–9). The Israelites decided to follow Joshua's leadership (Josh. 1:16–18). Next, Joshua secretly sent spies into the land to gather information about the nations that inhabited the land (Josh. 2:1). When the spies returned to Joshua, they said, "The Lord has surely given the whole land into our hands; all the people are melting in fear because of us" (Josh. 2:24). After Joshua received this information from the spies, he deliberately moved the Israelites into the promised land (Josh. 3:1).

Even though the story of Joshua took place thousands of years ago, strategic planning is still important. Today's leaders must be strategic in their planning, projecting potential outcomes, and gathering resources for adaptive change. Instead of trying to create the future, adaptive leaders respond to coming shifts, readying themselves and their organizations for probable future outcomes. This involves creating organizational strategies that focus on the entire organization in order to formulate strategic planning for the future (Corbin 2000: 13).

Many times, other team members see trends and sense necessary competitive moves before executive leaders detect them (Corbin 2000). Hughes et al. (2014) suggest that the Chief Executive Officer (CEO) is ultimately responsible for choosing the path of the organization. While this often involves some of the senior management in the decision-making process, it doesn't mean that these people are the only strategic leaders within the organization (p. 19). Organizations are increasingly calling for individuals at all levels to be strategic.

Leaders are decision makers for their organizations. Their decisions have a significant impact on the team and others, because they make decisions that impact daily operations, as well as short-term and long-term goals. A leader must become a strategist in order to move the organization into the future. Effective leaders make effective decisions (Hesselbein et al.

2006: 14). They are proactive, rather than reactive, in their decision making. Instead of merely being flexible and reacting to rapid change, great leaders will adapt and use proactive strategies (Corbin 2000). Even though the future is a moving target, it is necessary to plan for it. Leaders must use strategic planning to move the organization into a global community.

STRATEGIC LEADERSHIP

Every successful journey starts with an idea, but that idea must be cultivated with planning. Planning helps the visionaries to articulate their thoughts and bring them to fruition. Many organizations fail because they neglect to plan strategically. According to statistics published in 2017 by the Small Business Administration (SBA), "about one-fifth of business startups fail in the first year and about half of all employer establishments fail within five years; Only about one third survive ten years or more" (Schaefer 2018).

Why do most startup businesses fail? Multiple conditions cause these businesses to struggle and eventually go out of business (Schaefer 2018), but most come down to a lack of planning. Many small businesses fail because of fundamental shortcomings in their business plans. Success arises only for careful, methodical, strategic planning. A solid, strategic plan includes a description of the business, its vision and goals, keys to success, market analysis, potential problems and solutions, financial information, plans for budgeting and managing organization growth, as well as outlines for marketing, advertising, and promotional activities.

What is strategic leadership? Hughes et al. (2014) define strategic leadership as individuals and teams working together to create the direction, alignment, and commitment needed to achieve enduring performance potential for the organization (p. 11). It is the responsibility of leadership to create the momentum needed among their peers, to direct reports, and to motivate managers to inspire change. Strategic leadership requires individuals to continually think, reflect upon, and analyze all viewpoints and relationships that border their organization so that the organization's affluence is promoted and sustained (Sarfraz 2017). Strategic leaders must anticipate a wide range of scenarios. To do this, they must utilize all available information and trends, relying upon a broad network that allows them to analyze consumer, partner, and competitor perceptions. (Schoemaker et al. 2013).

Strategic leaders discover the obstacles, opportunities, and strengths within their organizations, and use the conclusions formed by themselves and others to make the best decisions (Gavetti 2011). Strategic leaders must analyze and rethink information in order to reveal concealed inferences and implications (Schoemaker et al. 2013). Careful evaluation of all this available information changes the leaders' outlooks. This helps the leaders become skilled in pinpointing ground for mutual understanding between themselves and board members, because they are open to multiple standpoints instead of being mired in a simplistic understanding of their options (Sarfraz 2017). Strategic leaders are on the lookout to inquire about and learn from the successes and failures of their own organizations, as well as that of their competitors, while inspiring other team members to do the same.

Strategic leaders navigate the challenges presented to them in order to create direction, alignment, and commitment and maximize organizational performance (Hughes et al. 2014).

They accomplish this by exercising the skills of strategic thinking, acting, and influencing. Strategic leaders use these skills throughout the cycle of learning to bring clarity and focus to strategy, enact that strategy with purpose and direction, and encourage others in their commitment to the future of the organization. Courageous leaders must implement this continuous process as they move the organization into the future. They must apply the skills of strategic thinking, acting, and influencing.

Strategic Thinking

Becoming an effective leader requires continuously improving strategic thinking skills, which builds competency in asking questions, anticipating, predicting, and making decisions. This ensures the viability of quality-driven cost-effectiveness for products and services (Randolph 2013). Strategic thinking is outcome-oriented and generates new ideas and alternatives (Tomey 2009). This type of thinking begins with asking the right questions: What is the impact of change on the organization? Are decisions based on interpretation of the past or anticipation of the future? What are the knowns that will influence the future?

An organization's performance is determined by strategic thinking, so having these essential traits, behaviors, and actions are imperative for leaders (How to enhance strategic thinking 2016). Strategic thinking involves the cognitive and social processes that lead to a shared understanding between the organization and its environment and using that understanding to set the direction for the organization's future (Hughes et al. 2014). Horwath (2008) notes that strategic thinking is the continual generation and application of business insight with the purpose of achieving competitive advantage (p. 1).

Strategic leadership, of course, involves strategic thinking, which must be intellectual, innovative, investigative, and collaborative. Strategic thinking also involves visioning, which emphasizes the importance of cooperation to develop and achieve the organization's vision. Strategic leaders must be aware of the business environment and the potential ways in which business and regulatory issues and trends might impact strategy development. This includes developing assessment and evaluation criteria based on economic, financial, customer, and industry metrics; these data can be used to identify opportunities with the most significant potential for business impact. Strategic thinking includes creating a strategy that aims toward the achievement of financial and other goals, and plan development, where data and previous procedures enable key priorities and objectives to be identified. Strategic leaders implement behaviors that pertain to goal achievement, communication of strategies, and alignment. This reflects the coordination of goals and plans in order to facilitate more efficient use of resources and compliance with external needs. Strategic thinking is an essential skill for courageous leadership, as it helps to align the organization's future direction (How to enhance strategic thinking 2016).

Strategic Acting

In most organizations, one of the most challenging aspects of strategic leadership is translating strategic thinking into actions (Hughes et al. 2014). Strategic acting is taking decisive action that is consistent with the organization's strategic direction, despite the ambiguity, chaos, and complexity inherent in organizational life. It involves translating thinking into priorities for collective action. Strategic acting is an opportunity for learning, because strategic decisions always involve uncertainty and adaptation, for this uncertainty naturally leads to ingenuity.

Hughes et al. (2014) note that strategic acting happens when resources such as money, time, energy, and personal or corporate reputations are committed to a project (p. 107). An organization simply having an idea about a product is entirely different from the organization acting to buy or sell that product. Chrysler CEO Lee Iacocca and Novak (1984) said, "You can use the fanciest computers to gather the numbers, but in the end, you have to set a timetable and act" (p. 50). Organizations around the world spend billions of dollars on leadership-development programs (Goldsmith 2006). They evaluate the effectiveness of the speakers but rarely are participants assessed based on the information they applied from the leadership-development program. People do not achieve a positive, measurable change in behavior because they go to classes and learn things; they get better only if they apply what they learn in training, and must be judged by the degree to which those around them are impacted.

Over time, organizations accumulate data relevant to the usefulness of theories and the validity of expectations and experiments, which are an opportunity for learning. "It has been said that anyone can think and act with the long-term in mind, or focus on the short-term imperatives, but it takes a special talent to be able to manage the tension between the two effectively" (Davies n.d.).

It is essential that the organization's short-term operational and strategic results are measured by both current performance and future capability (Davies n.d.). Strategic leaders follow these exercises in order to make a decision. First, they brainstorm the elements considered to be critical to organizational success; these are known as the strategic drivers. Second, they select the four or five drivers that are most critical to strategic success. Third, they post their selected drivers on a presentation board, and the team should sort them into logical categories. Once the team has decided on the key drivers, the team must set the importance of each driver, relative to other drivers. Finally, the group selects two or three drivers that combine the highest relative importance with the lowest current effectiveness. Strategic leaders will use these drivers to develop metrics for the assessment of future capability. Strategic acting is the organization setting clear priorities that have an enduring impact on all people throughout the organization (Hughes et al. 2014). It helps align the organizational ideas with key strategic drivers.

Strategic Influence

Strategic leaders must gain commitment from others; they must solicit support and dedication from the team. Strategic influence is how the leaders generate a commitment to the organization's strategic direction and learning, which is essential to sustaining competitive advantage in current organizations (Hughes et al. 2014). Organizations operate within a complex and chaotic environment, which makes it difficult for their leaders to set a plan, get others on board, and implement a strategy that is in congruence with their strategic planning.

Strategic influence is designed to not only inform but also change attitudes (Waller 2009). Strategic influence is a mindset that requires more than persuasion (Hughes et al. 2014). It starts with the leaders taking a hard look at themselves, which helps them reach beyond their comfort zone to establish relationships with others throughout the organization. They must have the competencies and mind-set to build trust, manage the political landscape, expand boundaries, solicit support, connect emotionally, and build and sustain momentum.

Leaders in middlemanagement also carry strategic influence. The ecological framework demonstrates how middle management affects the upward and downward strategic influence of the organizational alignment and external environment (Burgelman 1991, 1994). There are three levels of organizational problems: technical, managerial, and institutional. Middle management takes responsibility for managerial problems by mediating between its organization, customers, and suppliers (Thompson 1967). The middle-management strategic influence impacts the upward-management activities that have the potential to alter the organizational strategy by providing unique interpretations of emerging issues and providing new initiatives (Floyd and Woolridge 1997). Middle managers, as strategic leaders, help shape the organization's strategic thinking with the new initiatives that redefine the strategic framework (Bower 1970; Burgelman 1983). The middle managers' strategic influence affects the downward support by being Change Agents that foster adaptation and implementation of the organization's strategic plan.

As Change Agents, strategic leaders influence others by stimulating a culture that develops others, promotes learning, and increases team members' ability to adjust to change (Nonaka 1988, 1994). The leaders implement sets of ongoing intervention in order to bring the organization in alignment with strategy (Schendal and Hofer 1979; Nutt

1987; Sayles 1993). Strategic leaders have the potential to affect the organization's alliance with the external environment by injecting divergent thinking into the organization's strategy (Floyd and Wooldridge 1997). Strategic influencing connects with strategic thinking and strategic acting to build momentum for a strategic initiative. This requires a combination of reflection and analysis to understand why, when, and where to apply this skill (Hughes et al. 2014). The overlapping of strategic thinking, acting, and influencing does not happen by coincidence. Instead, they must complement each other if leaders and organizations are to enact strategy as a learning process.

Courageous Christian Leaders must develop a strategic mind-set in order to calculate risks and rewards by evaluating the organizational key drivers and selecting drivers of the highest priority in order to achieve organizational goals. Joshua, the leader of the Israelite military, had to strategically think, act, and influence others to follow God's plan for a brighter future. He made tough decisions, which affected the Israelites' future. Strategic leadership is not for the weak at heart, but for those who strive to change their organizations, cultures, and even the world. Leaders are asked to make decisions for the organization that have a significant impact on daily operations and long-term success, setting the tone for organizational direction, alignment, and commitment (Hughes et al. 2014). Planning requires leaders to think, act, and gain commitment from others in order to move the organization across cultural and geographical boundaries. The strategic leader uses the skills of strategic thinking, acting, and influencing throughout the life cycle of the organization to bring forth change within the organization and the surrounding environment. Strategic leadership changes others' attitudes and behaviors, building and sustaining momentum.

Chapter Four

Transforming the Organization's Culture

Joshua, the Israelite military leader, received spiritual authority from God to move the nation of Israel across the Jordan so they could possess the Promised Land (Josh. 1:1–3). God promised Joshua that He would be with him wherever he went and promised to never leave him as he led the Israelites to cross over the Jordan (Josh. 1:5). Hence, Joshua believed God and began to put a plan into action that led the Israelites to obtain their land. This meant they would stop wandering from place to place in the wilderness and finally possess a homeland. But with every promise fulfilled, there were obstacles and trials to overcome. Joshua had to gain support from the leaders of the Israelites in order to have a successful military campaign. This meant the leader had to buy into God's plan (Josh. 1:10–11).

Before Joshua spoke with the leaders about the change, the nation of Israel was in disarray. Moses, the previous military leader, was dead, and the Israelites mourned his death for thirty days. To add to their sorrow, the nation was trapped in the wilderness with no change in sight. They needed someone to come to their rescue. Joshua was the man God chose to finish Moses' assignment. Joshua gained support from the leaders, who promised to follow Joshua's leadership, just as they had followed Moses (Josh. 1:17).

Courageous Christian Leaders must engage in the strategic transformation of their organization's culture. Joshua had to get buy-in from the leading officers of the Israelites. The leaders had to accept the idea of moving across the Jordan in order to produce a change in the organizational culture. Organizational progress does not take place without resistance to change, because every culture has its ideas, values, and practices, while individuals within the organization form their own beliefs through their interactions with each other (Schein 2010). A successful organization requires leaders to create an organizational culture that aligns with organizational values and goals.

ORGANIZATION'S CULTURE

People are creatures of habit, and those habits form the behavioral patterns of individuals and groups. Culture consists of the learned beliefs, values, norms, symbols, and traditions that are common to a group of people; it's a shared quality of a group that makes them unique (Northouse 2013). Culture is a way of life, an amalgam of the customs, patterns, and "script" of a group of people (Gudykunst and Ting-Toomey 1988). An organization's culture shows people's interactions with each other: how they use the language, customs, and traditions that evolve, and the rituals they employ in a wide variety of situations (Goffman 1959, 1967; Jones et al. 1988; Trice and Beyer 1993; Van Maanen 1979). As individuals within the group interact with one another and with those outside the group, they set standards and values that create norms and practices for the group as they work together (Schein 2010). These norms and practices become endemic to the organization's culture. The organization develops espoused values, which it publicly announces as a goal to be achieved (Deal and Kennedy 1982, 1999).

The organizational climate is measured by the group members feelings toward each other as they interact and convey feelings about team members, customers, and others outside the group (Schein 2010). The group adopts embedded skills used to accomplish specific tasks, displaying unique competencies that require certain abilities, which are passed from generation to generation without necessarily being articulated in writing. As the group grows, and new members are accepted, the group shares cognitive frames that guide perceptions, thoughts, and language, which influence the new member's habits of thinking, mental models, and linguistic paradigms. Moreover, as the group continues to interact, it creates new understandings, which they expect others to accept as facts (Geertz 1973; Smircich 1983; Van Maanen and Barley 1984; Weick 1995; Weick and Sutcliffe 2001; Hatch and Schultz 2004). Culture informs members of who they are, how to behave toward each other, and how to feel good about themselves (p. 29). The three levels of culture—artifacts, espoused beliefs and values, and basic underlying assumptions—can be visualized and analyzed at various degrees.

Organizational Artifacts

Artifacts are the things individuals can see, hear, and feel when they encounter a new group with an unfamiliar culture (Schein 2010). The visible organizational products of the group are those such as the architecture of its physical building environment, its language, its technology and products, its artistic creations, and its style as embodied in clothing, manners of address, and emotional displays. Also, the group myths and stories, its published lists of values, and its observable rituals and ceremonies are visual products. The explicit culture manifests itself in the official organizational and communication structure (Cheung et al. 2011).

Organizational Espoused Beliefs and Values

Espoused beliefs and values originate from presuppositions and assumptions regarding what ought to be, in comparison to what it is (Schein 2010). Espoused beliefs and values are the groups' ideas, goals, values, and aspirations. These basic assumptions help to resolve challenges and overcome problems and issues. They will either work or not, but the assumptions that prevail ultimately become the organization's beliefs and values. The leader's personal values and assumptions combine with these organizational values to influence the group in adopting a certain approach to problems. As the group begins to accept the leader's assumptions as facts, they eventually become the group's espoused beliefs and values.

Organizational Basic Underlying Assumptions

Basic underlying assumptions develop when the group has succeeded in solving problems. As the group members repeatedly gain success from using the same approaches to solving problems, they begin to take these approaches for granted and assume that they will have success every time they are applied. Schein (2010) notes that, in this scenario, what once was a hypothesis, supported by a hunch or value, gradually comes to be treated as a reality (p. 27). These basic underlying assumptions reveal what the group truly believes and the learning process by which basic assumptions progress. The group believes its shared assumptions are the natural way to work. Organizational culture can also be evaluated by the extent to which the leader is effective and the organization is successful (Gordon and DiTomaso 1992). The leaders' understanding of the basic underlying assumptions of the group helps them get to the essence of the organization's culture and explain what is going on within it. Beneath the surface is the implicit culture that management and staff consider of real importance (Cheung et al. 2011).

CULTURE AND LEADERSHIP

Courageous Christian Leaders must think in a global context. While a global perspective creates new problems and issues to solve, leaders with the ability to decipher their culture are more likely to succeed. Culture is both a *here and now* dynamic phenomenon and a coercive background structure that influences us in multiple ways; it is reenacted continuously, created by our interactions with others, and shaped by our behavior (Schein 2010). A leader's ability to influence others' behaviors and values has the power to further develop an existing culture or form a new one. Cultures and leadership are intertwined because the organizational culture is embedded with the founders' beliefs and values. A value is an enduring belief that a specific mode of conduct or end-state of existence is personally or socially preferable to an opposite or converse mode of conduct or end-state of existence (Rokeach 1973: 5). The organization's values system is an interconnected network of belief concerning preferable modes of conduct or end-states of existence along a continuum of relative importance.

Organizational learning measures the degree to which the organization encourages innovation, gaining knowledge, and the development of individual and group capabilities. Leadership can influence culture by means of its characteristics or instrumental values (Cheung et al. 2011). Organizational leaders create artifacts that can be seen, felt, or heard when a group is encountered, but these artifacts are difficult to decipher (Schein 2010). Leaders will orchestrate the organizational climate by influencing a group of individuals to accomplish a goal (Northouse 2013). A shared vision should inspire a shared culture; both cultures should be willing to buy into and embrace whatever changes are necessary to strengthen and galvanize support from an organization's internal and external factors. Group learning develops from someone's original beliefs and goes through the process of creating cultures when individuals begin to adopt those ideas that work, which creates shared values and forms underlying assumptions.

ASSESSING VALUES

Values are the motivating factors that help bring a vision to reality (Hultman 2002). Rokeach's (1973) definition distinguishes between terminal values and instrumental values. Terminal values are things such as world peace, wisdom, and happiness; instrumental values focus on competence, which refers to one's ability or integrity (p. 5). An organization's internal culture and values may be misaligned with external markets, which can create problems to overcome for many organizations, especially organizations that desire to pursue opportunities abroad. With the advancement of technology, the world has become a smaller place in business, politics, and social constructs. How can an organization shift its focus and resources in order to take advantage of this opportunity? Global leadership is the answer. Leaders who possess global leadership skills are updated on the cultures they influence. Global leaders have competence in cross-cultural awareness and practice, possessing the skills to understand the business, political, and cultural environments worldwide. They are aware of the perspectives, tastes, trends, and technologies of other cultures (Northouse 2013). They can simultaneously work with people from many cultures and adapt to living in and communicating with different cultures from a position of equality rather than superiority.

A leader's ability to assess the values of his or her organization's culture is essential to creating shared values between merging cultures. Therefore, identifying an organization's underlying assumptions helps ensure that the organization remains true to its values. Hultman (2002) provides assessments for evaluating an organization's values, offering four criteria: balance, viability, alignment, and authenticity. These four criteria are designed to help fast-paced, energetic individuals and teams achieve their organization's goals without comprising organizational values (p. 97). Leaders must examine the organization's values in order to ensure that each value is given proper emphasis. This is referred to as balance.

Balance

Balance is the degree to which values are given proper emphasis relative to each other (Hultman 2002). The balance between opposites is a continuous variable. Standing for something is a clear sign of being against something else, but agreeing is not free of self-interest. Barrett (1998) notes that visionary organizations find a dynamic balance between the organization's needs for survival and growth, individual personal fulfillment, and communal and environmental sustainability (pp. 104–105). Leaders can contribute by helping individuals and the organization achieve balance.

Viability

Viability can be defined as the degree to which values are workable in the current business climate (Hultman 2002). Viable values must be based on accurate beliefs, be in tune with current realities, and produce the desired results. Values are not what we say, but what we do. Most of our spiritual, psychological, and social problems can be traced to a lack of integration and unity, both within ourselves and in relationships (Weisskopf 1959).

Alignment

Alignment is the degree to which compatibility exists

among values. There are two types of alignment: intrapersonal and interpersonal. Intrapersonal alignment is integration or congruence with a person's beliefs, values, and behaviors. They guide the person in one direction (Hultman 2002). Interpersonal alignment is consistency or integration among these variables at the interpersonal, team, and organization levels, also referring to the consistency between espoused and actual values. Senge (1990) notes that a shared vision is one to which many people are genuinely committed, generally because it reflects their own personal vision (p. 206). Manipulating others to accept shared organizational vision in order to gain alignment leads to passive-aggressive behavior, open defiance, sabotage, morale problems, and turnover. It is unrealistic to think that organizations will have 100 percent integration between team members to build complete trust.

Authenticity

Authenticity can be defined as the degree to which values are expressed (verbally or behaviorally) in a genuine, sincere manner. The authenticity of ideology (values and purpose) must be congruent with the ideology more than the content of ideology (Collins and Porras 1994). Authenticity values truth and is the criterion for the discipline of personal mastery (Hultman 2002). In order to cultivate authenticity, individuals must separate self-esteem from importance. A shared organizational commitment to values such as trust, mutual respect, honesty, openness, cooperation, collaborative partnering, and personal responsibility is essential to create a more authentic culture.

CREATING SHARED VALUES

Organizations with the opportunity to expand beyond their natural markets or globally are finding that they must adapt to managing certain tensions between local and global markets, between differentiated and integrated, and between many cultures and one organizational culture (Thomas et al. 2012). Accenture researchers interviewed forty CEOs and top leaders at multinational companies in order to investigate how they handled the creative tensions of competing on a global scale. There were three attributes repeatedly mentioned as improving the performance of top teams and their organizations: (a) a clear charter and operating principles; (b) the need to be swift about making decisions and who is included in decision-making processes; (c) the ability to "change ahead of the curve." Organizational leadership requires strategic planning, making good decisions, and navigating through challenging times to transform cultures. Organizations today are less hierarchical and bureaucratic than their predecessors; they focus primarily on gaining alignment around their organization's mission and values and empowering their followers to step up and lead rather than merely following rules and processes (Leavy 2015).

A leader's ability to communicate a shared vision is the starting place for creating a learning community. Communicating the organization's values, vision, and mission helps to inspire followers to complete their tasks and fulfill their personal goals. Kouzes and Posner (2012) share five exemplary principles that transform culture. They asked leaders from around the world to share what they did at their personal best in leading others. First, they were modeling the way. Second, they were inspiring a shared vision. Third, they were challenging the process. Fourth, they were enabling others to act. And fifth, they were encouraging the heart (p. 15). A leader's ability to set examples for others to follow is vital for others to accept or adopt a shared vision, providing examples of faith, trust, integrity, and commitment, which connect followers to leaders, helping to create a group that shares the same values. They must share a vision, rooted in the underlying assumptions of the group, into which followers will buy. The group members find their identity as they share experiences, which become presupposed beliefs (Schein 2010). A leader has the responsibility to create an environment of openness and collaboration, which inspires creativity within the group.

A leader's ability to create a shared culture between merging organizations must generate an atmosphere where groups can create new experiences, which forms new underlying assumptions. A leader's first approach should be to educate each member about the norms and assumptions of each culture, as knowing about other experiences helps individuals to understand others' behavior and eliminates myths about different cultures (Schein 2010). Leaders should also focus on cultural capacities and learning skills, also known as cultural intelligence. This develops understanding, empathy, and the ability to work with people from other cultures.

For leaders to work with different cultures, it requires four capacities: knowing essential information about other cultures; being culturally sensitive and mindful of other cultures; being motivated to learn about different cultures and behavioral skills; and flexibility to learn new ways of doing things (Schein 2010). Leadership's third approach should be to create a temporary island, which allows the groups to learn about each other and stimulates collaboration and trust. This forms shared experiences and, again, creates underlying assumptions. It also helps to confront the problems of authority, intimacy, and identity. Every group must work out its own identity, shared goals, mechanisms of influence, and strategies for managing both aggression and love through norms around authority and intimacy. Leaders have the privilege of forming beliefs, values, and standards that create or shape culture. These also develop as the group learns from new experiences. These values and experiences begin to transform organizational culture.

Cultures are dynamic relationships within organizations that compellingly affect the organizations and supersede all other performances. Organizations' cultures impact economic performance for long-term success (Schneider 2000). Organizational leadership creates core culture, intentionally or intentionally, by interactions, lifestyle, or ideas and through strategic planning. There are four essential principles that leaders can use to create a shared culture:

1) **Control**—People want certainty and predictability. Organizational cultures should be built around organizational goals and methods for achieving those goals.

2) **Collaboration**—Organizations are designed to be unified, which creates a synergy that brings a collection of ideas and experiences together. People feel more at liberty to share their thoughts when the organizational climate is open, transparent, and trustworthy. Collaboration helps to create a shared culture, where everyone's opinions, ideas, and suggestions are welcome.

3)**Competence**—Organizations are built around conceptual goal attainment. Shared cultures are formed when a group is knowledgeable about its tasks.

4)**Cultivation**—The connection between an organization's values and ideas in practice. The emphasis here is on what is being espoused, what is being put into operation, and the culture that emerges when centered on the attainment of conceptual goals.

SIX STAGES TO GAIN ORGANIZATIONAL BUY-IN

The process of creating and maintaining a healthy culture is complicated for most organizations, which is why many startup organizations lose the battle in the creating process. The approach to establishing a successful organization that breeds success requires courageous leaders who are intentional about the organizational culture. Getting the organization to buy into organizational goals or changes is essential and critical for success (Matthews and Crocker 2016). The term "buy-in" is prominent in popular trade publications and has many definitions in the changing literature. There are seven approaches for getting others to buy into change, including adapting your pitch, framing the issue, managing emotions, getting the timing right, involving others, adhering to norms, and suggesting solutions (Ashford and Detert 2015). Leaders recognize buy-in as a critical step in getting leadership to accept the use of social channels to connect with their support (Martin 2012). Obtaining participant buy-in is an important criterion of success, emphasizing the need to secure buy-in for implementation, instead of forced compliance.

The Transtheoretical Framework (TTF) emerged from a comparative analysis of eighteen leading approaches to therapy, which were later applied to a study of 872 individuals working to change their smoking behaviors (Prochaska and DiClemente 1982, 1983). The study reveals a deep understanding of how people make self-change, where individuals progress through a series of stages based on their level of motivation and cognition. Transtheoretical Framework (TTF) originated in the counseling and psychological disciplines, and its application in the organizational sciences is not novel (Matthews and Crocker 2016). The TTF could be used as a framework to explain and evaluate organizational change (Prochaska et al. 2001). TTF is illustrated by unlocking the cyclical diagram and laying the foundation for the six stages along with a series of experiences: denial, consideration, decision, action, sustainment, and resolution.

Denial

The first and most challenging stage to move an individual out is denial. When confronted with an organizational change, an individual who is in the denial stage of buy-in does not believe that the change is necessary or disagrees with the scope of the change (Matthews and Crocker 2016). The denial could be due to substantial investment in the status quo, a misunderstanding of the change, or a lack of clarity or communication regarding the initiative (Whelan-Berry et al. 2003). Or, admittedly, it could be due to the fact that the change is, in fact, a bad idea. This emphasizes the importance of listening and communication, rather than reliance upon top-down methodologies.

Consideration

The second stage on the continuum is "consideration." Consideration is defined as careful thought about something (Consideration 2015). The consideration stage involves the conscious consideration of the need to buy into the impending change. Individuals reaching this stage are no longer denying, disagreeing with, or avoiding the organizational change. They have begun to consciously think about whether they will buy in (Matthews and Crocker 2016). When considering whether to buy in, individuals are driven by several criteria, including benefits to self, benefits to others, approval from self, approval from others, costs and benefits, and disapproval from self and others.

Decision

Once individuals reaches the decision point of the continuum, they have consciously moved from only considering the costs and benefits of buying into the change effort involved in affirmatively deciding to buy in (Matthews and Crocker 2016). At the decision point, a sense of discrepancy has been built within the individuals, using targeted interventions, which has contributed to the understanding that their current state is less desirable than their future state as part of the change effort. In the decision stage, individuals begin actively planning how they will participate in the change effort, contribute to the change effort, and support the change effort. However, it is essential to understand that they have not taken any action, as they have only just decided that buying into the change brings more benefit than cost.

Action

The action stage of the buy-in continuum involves the individual engaging in required and requested change activities (Matthews and Crocker 2016). The action stage is the tipping point of the continuum, as the intrinsic motivation to buy into the change effort has reached a level that can be sustained with only minimal ongoing intervention. Thus, moving an individual to action is vital to change efforts, as resources such as individual coaching, mentoring, and performance management can be reallocated to those at lower levels of the continuum, once someone has reached this stage.

Sustainment

Once individuals reach the sustainment point of the continuum, they have primarily internalized the change effort as necessary and beneficial (Matthews and Crocker 2016). They continue to overtly act in support of the initiative through task completion and positive promotion and need little-to-no continued intervention to support their intrinsic motivation. The individual in the sustainment point has become firmly attached to the success of the change effort and is unlikely to regress to lower levels of the continuum without a catastrophic occurrence.

Resolution

Resolution is an essential point on the continuum, as it signifies the cognitive moment when the change effort is no longer an effort (Matthews and Crocker 2016). The change has become the new status quo, where the way of working and being within the organization is entrenched throughout the organizational culture. The cognition and behavior of the individual have resolved, and the old way of doing tasks no longer exists. Resolution is the end of the buy-in continuum, wherein the individual understands and accepts the new status quo and the change is installed. The buy-in is a decision-making process within which individuals can move back and forth across the continuum, according to their level of intrinsic motivation. Instead of relapse, this movement manifests itself as continuous progression and regression along the continuum.

CONCLUSION

Transforming an organization's culture is a daunting task for any leader, but strategic planning makes the change manageable. The leaders must evaluate the cultural climate in order to understand the organization's culture, strengths, and weaknesses. Organizational culture has artifacts, espoused beliefs and values, and underlying assumptions. The leaders must investigate down to the level of the underlying assumptions in order to decode the organization's culture so that they can know what the group truly believes and the learning process by which basic assumptions progress (Schein 2010). Decoding the basic underlying assumptions helps leaders know the organization's members are committed to putting into action the artifacts, espoused beliefs, and values of the organization.

Culture and leadership are interrelated. They depend upon each other to shape and develop the organization. Leaders influence culture, and culture influences the leaders' ability to lead successfully. Leaders must create a shared value that stimulates the organization to work as a team. The team members must buy into organizational ideas, values, and practices in order to maintain a healthy and sustainable culture. Everything takes place within an environment. Therefore, to produce a winning team, the organization's culture must resemble the success they desire. Joshua gained support from the leaders, who, in return, motivated the Israelites to cross over the Jordan River. The Israelites were able to receive their promise because they worked together as a team to achieve their shared vision (the Promised Land).

Chapter Five

The Essence of Leadership Spiritual Formation

Joshua's leadership success hinged on his willingness to read and meditate on God's law. Joshua recorded, "This Book of the Law shall not depart from your mouth, but you shall meditate on it day and night, that you may observe to do according to all that written in it" (Josh. 1:8). Joshua had to take the time to meditate on God's word day and night in order to gain a God-like mind-set. If Joshua desired to prosper and have success, he needed spiritual formation to transform his personal and professional life (Josh. 1:9). Joshua lacked the courage to overcome the fear that he faced off the other nations in the land of Canaan. Courage is an inner strength that produces virtue and formation (DeYoung 2013). The Christian form of this virtue acknowledges that no love is more powerful than

God's love. It is God's love that enables the greatest courage. Christ gave the most significant proof of His passion when He laid down His life for His friends (John 15:13).

The Courageous Christian Leader's spiritual formation is essential to personal, professional, and spiritual growth. There are emotional, mental, and physical prices to pay for leadership in the form of disappointment, dissatisfaction, and discouragement, which can even lead to hopelessness, anxiety, and depression. Leaders must expect some form of criticism from those who serve within the organization and from outside the organization. They can be criticized for their job performance and attacked for personal reasons. Leaders must be above the criticism, fatigue, loneliness, rejection, competition, and the abuse of power in order to effectively lead their organization (Engstrom 1976).

Leaders must be emotionally mature in order to lead effectively (Engstrom 1976). Engstrom notes that every good accomplishment has a price tag in terms of hard work, patience, faith, and endurance (p. 95). Courageous Christian Leaders must determine how much they are willing to pay for success by taking the time to think creatively and meditate. Many leaders think they are being inefficient when they make time for thinking and meditation. They, therefore, surge ahead without paying the price of thinking things through to determine the best process to meet their goals.

Over the last forty years, many organizations have experienced bad press because of immoral leadership behaviors. America has been rocked by financial and sexual scandals, at times involving some of the most potent and visible leaders in the world (The Barna Group 2002). The media has provided coverage of scandals involving Enron, Catholic priests, Tyco,

Martha Stewart, Arthur Andersen, Qwest Communications, WorldCom, and others. A small number of Americans retain high-level trust in leading cultural influencers, such as corporate executives, but The Barna Group (2002) reports that, for the most part, America's culture has a lack of confidence in organizational leadership:

> *Many Americans have lost faith in the leaders who are opinion shapers and cultural influencers. When asked to describe their level of confidence in seven types of influencers, only one of the seven teachers were awarded "complete confidence" or "a lot of confidence" by at least half of the public (53%). At the bottom of the list were executives of large corporations (12% had "complete" or "a lot of confidence" in them), followed closely by the producers, directors and writers of TV and films (13%), elected government officials (18%), and news reporters and journalists (20%). People made a clear distinction between their views of the executives of large corporations and those who own small businesses. The small businesses were given "complete" or "a lot of confidence" by 41% of the public; more than three times the level assigned to leaders of large businesses.* (The Barna Group 2002)

Organizational leaders fall from grace because they lack self-awareness, resulting in ethical blind spots—gaps between reality and an ideal (Bazerman and Tenbrunsel 2011). At the beginning of the American financial crisis that began in 2008, President Obama stated, "The recession was not caused by the normal downturn in the business cycle. It was caused by the perfect storm of irresponsibility and poor decision-making that stretched from Wall Street to Washington to Main Street" (p. 2). Richard Posner added, "The mistakes were systemic; the product of the nature of the banking business in an environment shaped by low-interest rates and deregulation rather than the antics of crooks and fools" (p. 2). Many factors led to these immoral practices and ethical failures (Thornton 2016). Often, the reasons for ethical breakdown within an organization are difficult to isolate, but several common culprits exist.

INDIVIDUAL BEHAVIOR THAT LEADS TO ETHICAL FAILURES

1. Ignoring boundaries (Ignoring ethics codes and organizational values that forbid an action).

2. Failing to use self-control (Willingness to take action, even though it's not allowed).

3. Entitlement view (A sense of deserving something, even though it's not allowed).

4. Warped personal values (A sense that something is permissible, even though it's not allowed).

5. Crowd-following (A belief that an action is permissible because others engage in it).

6. Lack of a moral compass (A belief that an action is permissible because it is not specifically prohibited).

ORGANIZATIONAL BEHAVIOR THAT LEADS TO ETHICAL FAILURES

1. Lack of clarity (What does ethical mean around here?).

2. No ethical leadership and behavior standards (There are no rules about this).

3. Oversimplified rules (Do the right thing).

4. Lack of positive role models (Who is doing it the right way?).

5. No training or coaching (How will I learn it?).

6. No accountability or enforcement (Even though it's not allowed, nothing bad will happen if I do it).

7. No performance integration (We say we want ethics, but we reward and promote based on the output).

8. Scapegoating (When problems happen, the blame is quickly passed around instead of anyone learning from their mistakes and fixing the culture.

Leaders and organizations both have blind spots that they ignore and deny. Many unethical behaviors go unnoticed because the organization focuses on other things instead of ethics (Bazerman and Tenbrunsel 2011). Organizations pay more attention to goals for which they receive rewards rather than unethical behaviors. Organizations reward individuals for noticing the unethical practices of others but overlook their own unethical practices. Leaders fail to notice unethical behavior when their environment fails to provide ethically appropriate consequences. People are also less likely to notice unethical behaviors that increase incrementally over time.

SPIRITUAL FORMATION

The word "spirituality" is a word used in many religious circles, which frequently speaks of a spiritual relationship with a deity (Johnson and Moore 2017). From African Animism to Zen Buddhism, various faiths express their relationships with a god as spirituality (Chan 1999; Demarest 2001; Bloesch 2007). In contemporary cultures, the word "spirituality" has expressed a wide variety of ideas, connected or unconnected with religion or belief in a god or gods. Therefore, it is essential to distinguish the Christian concept of spiritual formation from other ideas of spiritual formation. From a Christian perspective, spiritual formation is an ongoing process whereby the human spirit is transformed and molded to conform with the character of God (Willard 2006). It captures all the teachings, means, and disciplines directed toward deepening spiritual growth (May 1992).

Christian spiritual formation has been given a variety of names, such as discipleship, soul care, the pursuit of a deeper or higher life, sanctification, spiritual growth and maturation, and the development of spiritual intelligence (Johnson and Moore 2017). Christian spiritual formation is redemptive, grace-filled, and Spirit-guided, resulting in the ongoing process of sanctification, that is, the conformity of one's character to the image of Christ. This formation takes place in the heart (center of being), mind (center of thought), and hands (center of action) (Agnieszka Tennant 2005). Spiritual formation is redemptive—the restoration of something once possessed, lost, and regained. The heart of biblical faith is a narrative of transformation: from greatness to tragedy, to redemption. Spiritual formation is grace-filled and Spirit-guided. The Christian life from beginning to end is the work of grace in the heart. A leader's spirituality in this regard has to do with the nature of the leader's relationship with God, demonstrated through the process of transformation (John 4:24; Rom. 12:1–2; Matt. 5:9; Ps. 51:10). Transformation is a process started and performed by the Spirit, with which human beings cooperate. Change comes as the believer yields to the Spirit. Sanctification is the ongoing process that occurs in the life of the believer, from rebirth to the grave. This process then culminates in bodily resurrection and glorification.

The goal of spiritual formation is the conformity of one's character to the image of Christ—sins conquered, evil habits overcome, wrong dispositions and feelings rooted out, and holy tempers birthed and nurtured as believers trust God to work within themselves (Smith n.d.). This is a gradual, ongoing transformation (Johnson and Moore 2017). The specific objects of character formation are the heart, mind, and hand. The spiritual formation consists of heart-work and head-work directed toward the habituation of right actions. The Spirit transforms the distorted affections of the heart, the thinking of the mind, and behavioral predispositions of the Fall expressed in the works of the hands. The thirst for holiness expressed through full surrender opens one's life to transformation. The Holy Spirit purifies believers' hearts, renews their minds, and teaches them to act in ways consistent with God's Kingdom.

Christian spirituality for leaders involves a process of transformation, where leaders are nurtured and restored to wholeness in the image of God through a growing relationship with God in Christ, through the Holy Spirit (Scorgie et al. 2011). It's the process whereby God restores the leader through the work of the Holy Spirit. As the Apostle Paul states, "And we all, who with unveiled faces contemplate the Lord's glory, are being transformed into his image with ever-increasing glory, which comes from the Lord, who is the Spirit" (2 Corinthians 3:18). Transformation is for the spiritual life, where growth and development are for the physical life. Change in the spiritual life is a process of growth from a false identity into the identity of one in union with God.

Leaders Need Spiritual Direction

Christian spirituality poses its own beliefs about the nature of God, the nature of human beings, and the pathway that leads to the human–divine union (Buckley 1989). These beliefs are strained through the filter of history, tradition, culture, and personal religious experience to form the values of spirituality and the creative expressions of those values in various spiritual practices. The articulation of beliefs about God and human nature gives shape to the spiritual pathway through transcendence or immanence, whether God is perceived as beyond reach or experienced as close and intimate to human beings (Guardini 1962). God is a transcendent God who can be found within and around us, discernible in both a dramatic religious experience and in the pure, quiet love of a child for his or her parent (Nelson 2009).

Purpose of Spiritual Direction

Spiritual direction is not psychotherapy or pastoral counseling, even though healing can take place (Evans 2015). It is not the mutual friendship of two people who have a shared interest in spirituality, though they may encourage each other by their sharing. Spiritual direction is not an advice agency, where individuals are seeking advice, though Spiritual Directors can assist people in the discernment process. Furthermore, spiritual direction is neither coaching nor mentoring, even though personal growth, affirmation, decision making, and support may be a benefit of spiritual direction, which is not to say that the experiences of healing, affirmation, clarity, friendship, wisdom, compassion, and empathy will not occur during spiritual direction because they happen incidentally.

The primary benefit of spiritual direction is the ability to articulate one's experience of God to someone who will listen, observe, and understand (Evans 2015). The primary focus of spiritual direction is on people's relationships with God, helping them become more open to the promptings of the Spirit in the ordinary events of life (Wicks 1995). The process of spiritual direction summons people into continual conversion and toward a deepening union with God and communion with others, through the real presence of one person to another.

The Process of Spiritual Direction

Spiritual direction is a process under the rule of Spirituality, and its foundation is theology (Schneiders 1989; Evans 2015). Those who practice spiritual direction believe that God has a relationship with human beings and desires to relate personally to them whether they know it or not (Birmingham and Connolly 1994). The Center for Religious Development, for example, articulated its theological presuppositions regarding spiritual direction. It believes that spiritual direction does not start or shape a person's spiritual development but that God has already been acting in a person's life. The center also believes that spiritual direction will benefit people who are aware of God's work in their lives and who want a more explicit relationship with God. Spiritual direction is therefore predicated upon the belief that God communicates in all life experiences (Edwards 1983; Palmes 1996).

Christians' Acceptance of Spiritual Direction

In the 1400s, Catholic leaders had externally rejected the

Reformation, but the need for church reform continued to be internally expressed many times: The councils of Constance (1415), Basel (1439), and the Protestant at Worms, Nuremberg, Speyer, and Augsburg continued to fight for internal reformation (Houston 2008). In 1546, the council of Trent reached a compromise that allowed dogma and church reform to be handled in alternating sessions. One of the first outcomes was the adoption of the Jesuit order under Ignatius of Loyola (1491–1556) and the acceptance of his "Spiritual Exercise," which he completed by 1548. Ignatius implemented a method of examining one's conscience, of meditating, praying, and contemplating to get rid of disordered affections before God (Ivens 1998). The spiritual direction of Ignatius is still identified with the medieval church, but now with new mobility in both geographical and moral fallacy; geographical, spiritual direction moved beyond the monastic life and moral inconsistency around the sacrament of penance.

True sorrow is motivated by the fear of God and results in true repentance, which arises from the human capacity to receive grace and experience love (Houston 2008). How can fear and love be measured and distinguished? Ignatius concludes his Spiritual Exercises with "Rules of Discernment" by stating, "Given that the motives of pure love in the constant service of God our Lord valued above all; nevertheless, we ought to greatly praise the fear of the Divine Majesty" (p. 93). Ignatius's frequent use of "Spiritual Exercises" communicated what he meant by constant service to God our Lord. He was claiming the division between proponents of attrition (sorrow) and contrition (repentance) to be resolved by doing the Spiritual Exercises.

Ignatius's primary concern was the welfare of individuals;

every month, he wrote to each of his leaders. He was concerned with the conversion of the person rather than with a public renunciation of secular society. He desired for the person to become Christ-like, rather than to belong politically to Christendom (Caraman 1990). Christians seek to be authentic and independent of institutional religious life that spiritual direction now will tend to promote (Houston 2008). Beginning from the time of Martin Luther, and then Ignatius and Calvin, a succession of both Catholic and Protestant leaders from the sixteenth century to the nineteenth century wrote large collections of pastoral letters, making of the genre a great instrument of soul care and direction. "The difference was that while the Catholic's priestly authority was more 'directive' and conscious of belonging to various 'schools' of founding leaders, the Protestant ministries of 'soul care' were more diffused, suggestive, and shepherding" (p. 94). The cultural revolution in the nineteenth century led to the expression of Romantic culture.

Today's quest for authenticity is much more complicated and related to a purer narcissism of "seeking what is best for me." The religious groups were affected by this movement (Houston 2008). The expression is believing, but not belonging, so the idealistic Christians no longer attend church, a habit which they claim to be authentic in their own eyes. This shift from elite culture into the mass culture is now moving again into the age of authenticity, which seeks deeper self-identity (Taylor 2007). The quest for authenticity is crossing the former church and divides in many ways. The focus today is on individuals and one's spiritual experience, with caution expressed toward institutional authority. The quest for being oneself, indifference to denominational boundaries, and institutional disagreement are generating new religious mobility, which has intensified the need for spiritual direction and soul care like never before.

The Apostle Paul provides advice, instruction, and encouragement to Christians who are trying to live out the gospel in different and hostile environments (Currie 2006). Pauline instruction is called "Paraenetic," in that it contains a series of appeals, both positive and negative, which speak to the life that is shared by those who worship Jesus Christ as Lord. These admonitions and words of encouragement are deeply related to the gospel Paul was proclaiming, and are expressed in his instructions to the Thessalonian church.

Paul employs parental metaphors and situates himself above the Thessalonians, but his use of the term (ἀδελφοί) shows that he is also in solidarity with his converts (Burke 2012). On two occasions, he addresses the Thessalonians as siblings (1 Thessalonians 5:12, 14), with the implication being that he is their brother. However, Paul is somewhat reluctant about this and stops shy of ever going as far as to say the latter. The reason for this is that Paul never uses his most frequent designation for Christians, the sibling metaphor, for himself; he never calls himself their sibling in the letter. Paul is the Thessalonians' parent (mother and father), and they are his children and his brothers. Such a distinction is echoed by Aristotle, for whom the father is a full head and shoulders above his children but is not unlike an elder brother to them (Burke 2012).

Romans 12:9–13 and Philippians 4:4–7, constitute the heart of this passage. Paul's life as he describes it is the life found in the crucified and risen Lord (Currie 2006). Forgiveness ceases to be something merely lovely when it is lavished upon us at the foot of the cross. Forgiveness is something that can only then be extended to others when offered ungrudgingly and out of the joyful supply that made possible "in Christ Jesus for you" (v. 18). Here "joy" (chara) and "grace" (charI) share more than just the same etymological root: they both describe a Christological reality that is scary in its goodness.

Christians have accepted Apostle Paul's prayer for the Thessalonians, "May the God of peace sanctify you entirely; and may your spirit and soul and body be preserved blameless at the coming of our Lord Jesus Christ" (1 Thess. 5:23). Origen followed a tripartite scheme of the human being, but later the Father's "heart" and "soul" overlapped. Those influenced by Neo-Platonism saw the "soul" itself as tripartite, consisting of memory, mind, and will (Houston 2008). In the Middle Ages, Thomas Aquinas applied the Aristotelian theory of form and matter to provide the key to the relationship between the body and the soul, the latter being the agent of the intellect. The Renaissance revived the centrality of the soul, but the adverse reaction to the Reformation resulted in a renewal of skepticism, especially in France, until the Enlightenment, when the thinking self-replaced the soul.

Applying Spiritual Direction

Spirituality has a variety of meanings and references to different enterprises; it is a personal experience, Christian teaching, and writing or academic study (Principe 2000). The focus of the spiritual life may be oriented toward God (supported by theology), toward the world (related to nature and ecology), or toward people (found in human potential). Spirituality is the person's life lived in harmony with the Spirit of God (Ault 2013). Spirituality is the transformational discovery of a person's correct response to God's call into the adventure of incarnation, which is not a private relationship, but a relationship involving other people (Mcintosh 1998). Christian spirituality, as lived within the Body of Christ in response to God's call, embraces all dimensions of a person's life with its complexities and multiple relationships. The invitation into the adventure of incarnation provides the background for spiritual direction.

Spiritual direction focuses on the maintenance and development of spiritual health and well-being. The underlying goal of spiritual direction is to develop the directee's relationship with God. Prayer is critical to this relationship, which includes both conversational and meditative or centering prayer (Sperry 2003). Spiritual direction involves a trained director who guides another person called the directee. The director listens with sensitivity to the directee's life story, using spiritual discernment to understand the movement of God in the directee's daily life. The relationship in Christian spiritual direction is triadic, which involves the director, the directee, and God, the Holy Spirit. Intervention in spiritual direction includes prayer and other spiritual practices. Under the care of the Holy Spirit and the activation of counsel, different things happen in the ministry of spiritual direction at different times (Wicks 1995). These include:

1. Listening in order to unfold the mystery of a personal relationship with the Lord and others.

2. Clarifying a person's likeness to God's image: The whole shape and orientation of a person's spirituality is profoundly affected by the operative image of God in that person's life.

3. Helping people to clarify the experience: Helping the directees reflects on their growth through grace and faith.

4. Identification and clarification of a person's value system: Directees grow to the extent that they live congruently with their value systems.

5. Affirmation: An essential function of the director is to affirm the directee in his or her giftedness.

6. Challenge: The discovery and development of charism presume not only affirmation but also testing for validation.

7. Discernment: A key activity of the director should be to describe things under the explicit rubric of spiritual discernment.

8. Teaching: There may be areas where there are gaps in a person's understanding of issues related to growth.

9. Integration: Helping persons to integrate their lives so they can make positive changes.

10. Accountability: Checking in with a guide can help a person avoid some of the pitfalls that come with unaccompanied self-assessment.

11. Help through the desert and darkness: There are times for all persons seeking spiritual depth when they experience the dryness of the desert and the onslaught of the demonic. The spiritual director must guide during this time.

12. Prayer: Last among the dynamics of spiritual direction is praying with and for the person coming for direction.

CONCLUSION

Spiritual direction is a process that leads a person to a closer relationship with God. During the process of spiritual direction, the director guides the directee to identify and clarify his or her spiritual relationship with God. Leaders are often called upon to help followers with their spiritual imperfections. Christian spirituality is a sincere belief and commitment to Christ, the Son of God. It is the worship of the incarnated, crucified, and risen Christ. The goal of Christian spirituality is transformation, to bear the image of Christ (Col. 1:15). Spiritual direction is necessary for Christian Leadership because Christian spiritual formation is needed for today's leaders. The challenges of leadership can sometimes be daunting for leaders. Therefore, leadership requires Courageous Christian Leaders to endure hard times in order to see their assignment completed. Christians must depend on Christian spiritual formation to experience the redemptive, grace-filled and Spirit-guided hand of a loving God, and go through the sanctification process, which is designed to transform the leader's character into the image of Christ (Agnieszka Tennant 2005).

Chapter Six

The Kingdom of God and Jesus' Leadership

Courageous Christian Leaders must follow Jesus' leadership to implement God's kingdom's mission. God chose many leaders to lead His people. God chose Joshua, as well as Jesus, to fight against those who oppose God's plan for redemption. Jesus provides leadership examples through His life experiences and interactions with His disciples. Jesus was a Visionary, Strategist, and Servant Leader. He depended on the guidance of the Holy Spirit to help bring the Kingdom of God into existence. God called John the Baptist to announce the arrival of God's Kingdom and introduce Jesus as the Messiah (Matt. 4).

John the Baptist came preaching in the wilderness of Judea and saying, "Repent, for the Kingdom of heaven is at hand!" (Matt. 3:1–2). Many came to John in the wilderness, inquiring about the Kingdom of God and water baptism (Matt. 3). John prepared the way for the people to receive Jesus Christ the Messiah. John encouraged them to forsake the corrupt world and be transformed by changing their minds and lives. This meant a change of heart, a turning of the whole person to God and His offer of forgiveness and mercy (Gleeson 2016). For Jesus' immediate hearers, it meant becoming a renewed people of God, a Kingdom people, and a people who would give up their agendas and trust Jesus to bring His Kingdom and the Kingdom's plan into reality.

Jesus was telling them to abandon their crazy dreams of nationalist revolution against the offensive, occupying Roman power. It is the most grandiose vision that the world has ever known. Jesus' love and affection for His Father created His passion for seeing God's will come to fruition. This sacrificial lamb produces life for everyone who receives Him. God's redemption plan introduced the Kingdom of God's message, the Gospel. Jesus' ministry begins with these words, "Repent, for the Kingdom of God is at hand" (Matt. 4:17), and He shared with His disciples the things about God's Kingdom during His last forty days on earth (Acts 1:3).

JESUS' MISSION ON THE EARTH

Jesus' mission in life was to do the will of God the Father (John 6:38). He did not come to build His Kingdom, but to advance God's Kingdom. He taught His disciples to pray that God's Kingdom would come, and that God's will would be done on earth as it is in heaven (Matt. 6:10). God's Kingdom's agenda is to bring peace, joy, and hope to a dark world, and the only remedy for this darkness is light. Jesus is the Light of the world that shined in a dark place, but the darkness did not comprehend the light (John 1:5). The religious leaders sought to kill the Light, rather than embrace Him. The image of companionship in the kingdom of God reflects the radical nature of the table fellowship of Jesus and the mission He passed on to His disciples (Vondey 2008). The New Testament portrays the entrance to the wedding feast as happening both by God's choice and by the right earned by those who make their way to the table. Christ promised to give the hidden "manna" to those who conquer death (Rev. 2:17). The manna is the invisible Bread (Jesus) that came down from heaven, which provides eternal life for the faithful stewards.

The Good and Faithful Servant

Jesus desires faithful and wise servants to help carry out the Great Commandment and the Great Commission. These individuals are Believers; their mission and witness are a vital concept for the church and involve all members (Karkkainen 2002). All believers are classified as priests who have responsibilities inside God's kingdom.

Jesus gives all Believers gifts. These gifts are designed to be used to advance God's Kingdom's agenda. Matthew, chapter twenty-five, records Jesus teaching a parable to His disciples about the Kingdom of heaven, in which the master called three servants and gave them gifts according to their abilities (Matt. 25:14–15). Each one of the servants had a responsibility to complete. They had to produce a profit for the master. The servant who failed to provide a gain was labeled as a lazy and wicked servant because he was unable to follow the master's orders (Matt. 25:26). But the ones who produced a profit for the master were labeled as good and faithful servants (Matt. 25:23).

Christian churches throughout the world must not merely share their lives and God's word with one another, but they need to get out of their little fishbowls and manifest the presence of Christ through their words and lives (Beale 2004). The Christian must present God as the God of generosity who desires all to be redeemed by the blood of Jesus. God in Creation gave the physical universe its nature, and He gave human beings their lives, but with the acts of calling Israel and becoming incarnated, we learn that God created us to have a life with Him. Human beings share the divine presence with God beyond human existence; this is divine generosity (Allen and Springsted 2007). The world needs to see God as Redeemer through Christ, which is God's Redemption plan for the world. "For God so loved the world that He gave His only begotten Son, that whoever believes in Him should not perish but have everlasting life" (John 3:16). Jesus said to His disciples, "The harvest indeed is plentiful, but the laborers are few" (Matt. 9:37). God's Kingdom's agenda of love, redemption, and restoration must be shared with a lost world.

Jesus encouraged His disciples to focus on using their resources to help advance God's Kingdom. He spoke of the returning Son of Man, coming in His glory with all the holy angels, after which, He will sit on the throne of His glory (Matt. 25:12). All the nations will be gathered before Him and separated from one another, as the shepherd divides his sheep from goats (Matt. 25:32). All will be judged based on their faithfulness to serve in God's Kingdom. Those who were called faithful will receive eternal blessings, but those found unfaithful will receive eternal damnation. They will be blessed or cursed based on their relationship with Jesus (Matthew 25:14–46)

Jesus' Relationship to God's Kingdom

John the Baptist baptized Jesus, and the Spirit led Him into the wilderness to be tested by Satan, during which time Jesus experienced a variety of temptations (power, wealth, security) by Satan (Matt. 4:1–11). But during His greatest trial, He received the grace, blessings, and care of the angels who looked after him (Matt. 4:11). Jesus came out of the wilderness, "filled with the power of the Holy Spirit" (Luke 4:14), fired up to preach and witness to the Kingdom of God (Mark 1:15). Jesus dedicated His life to God's Kingdom's message (Goldman 2010). The message of God's Kingdom was so important to Jesus that He taught His disciples about God's Kingdom repeatedly, in multiple parables and sermons. However, Jesus' message and witness to the Kingdom of God's power was so alien to human understanding of power that the disciples struggled to grasp His meaning. The Church, down through the ages, has likewise struggled to understand, even remember, the primary position of the Kingdom of God in its life. Jesus' relationship with God as a father signifies the closeness and intimacy of their relationship. Jesus called God his "Abba," or "Father." The experience of God as Abba captures the longing of humans to rest in God's love, the desire to feel the fullness of living, moving, and being in God (Fullenbach 2002). Jesus' life is defined by his relationship with God and His vision and experience of the Kingdom of God. The Kingdom of God is both of this world and the world after. The Kingdom of God is a world of peace, justice, forgiveness, and reconciliation, where all humanity and creation are given dignity and respect and are embraced in love and with joy.

God's Kingdom Is a Community

The Kingdom of God is a community of people who are called the Church, which is the body of Christ. This community was formed as a result of Jesus' work of redemption (Vorster 2015). The Church is sent into the world to proclaim the message of hope. The people who are going out into the world no longer adhere to the sinful structure of the world (Harvie 2009). The Church lives the eschatological in its message of hope and as God's sanctified people. The Church is an institution of the Kingdom of God that began with Christ. If history lasts, the Church is not identical to the Kingdom of God, because the Church ends with the coming of Christ and the last judgment (Rahner 1975).

The Church Is the Herald of God's Kingdom

The Kingdom of God lies at the heart of Jesus' proclamation and life (Goldman 2010). Jesus' proclamation of the Kingdom is what ignited His mission and what led to His death. From the beginning of Jesus' public life and His time in the wilderness, filled with the Holy Spirit, he summarized His mission by drawing from the prophet Isaiah. Jesus said,

> *The Spirit of the Lord is upon me because he has anointed me to bring good news to the poor. He sent me to proclaim release to the captives and recovery of sight to the blind, to let the oppressed go free, to proclaim the year of the Lord's favor* (Luke 4:18–19).

Jesus kept pointing to clues of where the Kingdom was breaking through into the here and now. When the Church is focused on the Kingdom of God, it has its eyes on the poorest of the poor in local and global communities. The people of the Kingdom give financially and give their time to activities that work to alleviate material suffering, but also to develop relationships throughout all strata of society. Jesus' mission became the Church's mission, which is the Kingdom's vision and message of hope, peace, and the redemption of humanity.

JESUS, THE VISIONARY

Jesus was able to see people's hurt and pain. He was moved with compassion because the people around him were weary and scattered (Matt. 9:35–36). They were people without any spiritual leadership, so Jesus encouraged His followers to pray that God would send some help to take care of the people (Matt. 9:37–38). Jesus stood in contrast with the rigid social boundaries of the Jewish social world—boundaries between the righteous and the outcast, men and women, rich and poor, and Jews and Gentiles (Borg 1987). Jesus' vision invited people to escape the world of destruction and enter the narrow gate that leads to life and peace (Matt. 7:13–14). Ford (1991) believes that leaders' effectiveness depends on their abilities to judge objectively and reach measurable goals (p. 105). Jesus provides answers to people's spiritual condition. To those who are broken, without hope, and lacking in spiritual discernment, Jesus says, "Hearing you will hear and shall not understand and seeing you will see and not perceive; for the hearts of this people have grown dull" (Matt. 13:13).

JESUS' VISION IS SPIRITUAL

Jesus' leadership began with the vision of the Kingdom of God. Jesus' vision was spiritual; He spoke in a parable to His disciples, describing "the secret of the Kingdom of God" (Ford 1991: 105). Jesus' ability to live by the unseen was a great asset to His leadership. Jesus communicated God's Kingdom as a plan of redemption, love, and hope for a dying world. Jesus committed His life to this vision and eventually died for what He believed (Gleeson 2016). He compellingly communicated this vision, and many of His followers today share His faith vision and faith commitment. Jesus' vision of God's Kingdom included all human beings, with the fulfillment of the deepest aspirations of the human heart, and God's plan for all creation. Jesus' teachings point to the present fact and the future existence of the Kingdom of God (Vorster 2015). Christianity stands and falls with the reality of Jesus' resurrection from the dead by God and His vindication of the powers of this earth (Moltmann 1965). The event of Jesus' resurrection from the dead became a new reality of the Kingdom of God in world history but will reach its fulfillment with the end of human history (Ridderbos 1950).

Jesus' Vision Is Practical

Jesus' vision was not religious. Instead, His vision was practical and down to earth; His vision was a way of seeing life lived out in the reality of God (Ford 1991). Christ did not only relate to the religious and church matters, but He also looked at everything through the eyes of God. Whether one's profession is that of a doctor, lawyer, scientist, salesperson, janitor, teacher, or pastor, all are important in God's Kingdom. Jesus' purpose was to bring abundant life to His followers (John 10:10). His vision inspired a common goal—a vision that people wanted to make into a reality (Kouzes and Posner 2012).

Jesus' Vision Solves Problems

Jesus' vision was compelling and provided solutions for everyday problems. Jesus shows His followers that God is the total answer to all needs (Ford 1991). Jesus called ordinary men to become fishers of men, to drive out evil spirits, and to heal many diseases. His Kingdom was the Kingdom that provided an answer for all their problems; it offered teaching for the ignorant of mind, deliverance for those oppressed spiritually, healing for the diseased, forgiveness for sinners, and reconciliation for all. The gospel message starts with Jesus proclaiming, "God so loves the world" and culminates with a beautiful plan for its total redemption.

Jesus' Vision Is Personal

Jesus' vision is personal; He focuses on people. His vision's purpose was to engage every single human being. Jesus' conversation with Zacchaeus shows God's love for people who didn't know their identity in God. Jesus met Zacchaeus as he traveled through the territory of Jericho (Luke 10:1–6). Zacchaeus was a tax collector who was short in stature, and he climbed a tree to see Jesus as He passed by. He had defrauded many citizens out of money (Luke 10:7–8). Although he was a descendant of Abraham, he didn't understand his covenant relationship with God, so Jesus came to restore Zacchaeus to his right relationship with His heavenly Father (Luke 10:9–10). Jesus looked through the Father's eyes, and He saw a vision of God's power working through individual people (Ford 1991).

Jesus' vision is closely related to His relationship with His Father. He taught His disciples to pray that God's Kingdom would come and that his will would be done on earth as it is in heaven (Matt. 6:9–15). Jesus only says and does what His Father desires. He sought to obey God's will (John 12:49; John 4:34).

Jesus, the Strategist

Jesus' strategy centered on God's Kingdom's ideas. His primary goal was to seek the Kingdom of God. Jesus' message was God's blessings to help overcome obstacles despite current life experiences. He continued to tell the crowd that they were blessed if they would accept God's Kingdom's principles for living. Matthew records Jesus' message to the crowd,

> *Blessed are the poor in spirit, for theirs is the kingdom of heaven. Blessed are those who mourn, for they shall be comforted. Blessed are the meek, for they shall inherit the earth. Blessed are those who hunger and thirst for righteousness, for they shall be filled. Blessed are the merciful, for they shall obtain mercy. Blessed are the pure in heart, for they shall see God. Blessed are the peacemakers, for they shall be called sons of God. Blessed are those who are persecuted for righteousness' sake, for theirs is the kingdom of heaven. Blessed are you when they revile and persecute you and say all kinds of evil against you falsely for My sake. Rejoice and be exceedingly glad, for great is your reward in heaven, for so they persecuted the prophets who were before you* (Matt. 5:1–12).

Jesus infiltrated the world of others by communicating the ideas of another kingdom (Ford 1991). He shared a new vision for the world, a message that is essential to change people's path for the future. Jesus encouraged His disciples to "follow me, and I will make you fishers of men." This meant he wished His followers to be with Him for hours and hours, for days and days, and that their relationships would be transformed because of the relationship they shared with Him. Again, Jesus' strategy for leadership was to seek first God's Kingdom, and not the kingdom of leadership; seeking God's rule, not human domination. People matter most to God. They are not a technique. The heart of leadership is not in mastering the "how to," but in being mastered by the amazing grace of God.

Jesus' strategy for transforming the world was to transform the heart of each person:

> To the politician, Jesus says, "Those aren't just voters you solicit; they are people that God loves." To the doctor and social worker, he says, "Those aren't just casing you see; they are persons that Christ came to set free." To the preacher, he says, "That is not just an audience to listen to your words; those are the blind I came to give sight." To the teacher he says, "Those students aren't names in a computer; they are a person made to know God and His truth forever (p. 76).

Jesus aimed to extend the rule of God to all nations and to set people free from all that binds them (Ford 1991). He is accomplishing this by a radical transformation in the hearts of people who know they are in need and who are willing to be changed. Jesus, as a strategist, worked to launch the Kingdom of God into the culture. Jesus went throughout Galilee, teaching in their synagogues, preaching the gospel of the Kingdom, and healing all kinds of sickness and disease among the people (Matt. 4:23). People from all around the region came to Jesus to be healed of various diseases; he delivered the epileptic, the paralytic, and the demon-possessed from their afflictions

(Matt. 4:24). Great multitudes followed Him from Galilee, and Decapolis, Jerusalem, Judea, and beyond the Jordan (Matt. 4:25). Dale (2006) notes seven strategies Jesus implemented to launch the Kingdom of God. He believes Jesus focused on defining Himself, building a new community, training apprentices, selecting the right times and places for action, mobilizing His followers, modeling love, and taking risks to succeed (pp. 23–25).

Jesus Defining Himself

Leaders throughout history have had to define themselves. Moses, Paul, Martin Luther, and John Wesley all defined themselves by leading through a critical time. They all waited to take up leadership roles until they were approximately thirty years of age (Dale 2006). It takes maturity and mileage to prepare for ministry and strategic leadership. Jesus also started His ministry at the age of thirty. He spent years working with His hands as a carpenter and caring for His mother and siblings. These experiences, along with His understanding of Scripture, helped shape His strategy for ministry and leadership.

Jesus Building a New Community

Jesus called twelve individuals to join forces with Him to spread the message of the Kingdom of God. Jesus was building a new community that would later lead His Church. He called His disciples to go into the world and make disciples of all nations and teach them to observe all things that He had commanded them, and He promised to be with them until the end (Matt. 28:18–20). He created an extended family that bonded together, saying, "Whoever does the will of God is my brother and my sister and mother" (Mark 3:35). Jesus called for His followers to be committed to Him as to a family member.

Jesus Training His Apprentices

Jesus called His disciples to be learners. His message to His disciples and the multitudes he taught was how to live in the Kingdom of God and how to be led by God's Kingdom's influence (Matt. 5–7). Dale (2006) notes that those who heard the Sermon on the Mount, who listened to Jesus' parables and observed his miracles were receiving on-the-job training for Kingdom building (p. 24). Jesus received instruction from His Father. He did not do anything outside of God's plan. Jesus said, "Most assuredly, I say to you, the Son can do nothing of Himself, but what He sees the Father do; for what He does, the Son also does in like manner" (John 5:19). He displayed a keen sense of timing. He knew when His time arrived to be known as the Messiah. He would not allow His followers to announce his Messiahship until the proper time. He knew His departure time from the earth, and he deliberately traveled to an area of Samaritan territory to show the love of God to a diverse people who experienced prejudice and hate from the Jews.

Jesus Mobilizing His Followers

Jesus mobilized His twelve disciples to go to the Israelites to preach the good news of the Gospel and heal the sick (Matt. 10:5–8). He also appointed the seventy disciples to go out two by two to every town and place where He had planned to go, sending them out as lambs among wolves (Luke 10:1:3). After His resurrection and before His ascension to heaven, Jesus commanded His disciples to wait in Jerusalem until they received power from the Holy Spirit to be His witnesses in Jerusalem, Judea, Samaria, and to the ends of the earth (Acts 1). He sent the Apostle Paul to carry His message of grace to Gentiles, kings, and the Israelites (Acts 9:1–15).

Jesus Modeling Love

Jesus' message was love. He lived, taught, and preached about love and the Kingdom of God. The overarching theme of the Holy Scriptures is love. Jesus said, "For God so loved the world that He gave His only begotten Son, that whoever believes in Him should not perish but have everlasting life" (John 3:16). He gave His disciples the greatest commandment, which is to "love the Lord your God with all your heart and love your neighbor as yourself" (Matt. 22:37–40). Even as Jesus hung on the cross, He asked God to "forgive them because they do not know what they do" (Luke 23:34). Jesus communicated and demonstrated the love of God wherever He went.

Jesus Taking Risks to Succeed

Jesus' gospel message is built on the idea of exercising faith in order to achieve success in God's Kingdom's economy. The Holy Scriptures record that without faith it is impossible to please God, for whoever comes to Him must believe that He is a rewarder of those who diligently seek Him (Heb. 11:6). Faith involves risk, but if one never applies faith, that person will never achieve God's success. To be faithful requires one to take the risk. Throughout history, missionaries remind believers to expect great things from God by attempting great things for God; if we don't try, we will fail for sure; if we do try, the risk that we take has the potential to lead us to success. This is why Paul reminds the church to walk by faith and not by sight (2 Cor. 5:7).

JESUS TAUGHT HIS FOLLOWERS SERVANT LEADERSHIP

Jesus taught His disciples the essence of leadership. These men were called to help fulfill the Great Commandment and the Great Commission. They were from various backgrounds and had different life experiences, but Jesus discerned each one of their hearts and invited them to follow Him. Clarke (2008) notes that the language of serving and servanthood has long been associated with Christian leadership, after the pattern of Jesus (p. 98). The gospel according to Mark records Jesus saying, "You know that those who are considered rulers over the Gentiles lord it over them, and their great ones exercise authority over them" (Mark 10:42). Here, Jesus references the hierarchy model of leadership, which he denounced. He continues, "Yet it shall not be so among you, but whoever desires to become great among you shall be your servant" (Mark 10:43). Jesus desired His disciples to take the servant-leadership role. The apostles also identified themselves as slaves or bondservants for Christ. They served humanity with an attitude of humility.

Servant Leadership

Servant Leadership is one of the models of leadership that can be implemented to establish the Kingdom of God. The servant leaders must cast God's Kingdom's vision to their followers. Kouzes and Posner (2012) suggest that the leaders must engage others to join in a cause and to want to move decisively forward (p. 139). The leaders must help the followers see and feel how their interests and aspirations are aligned with the vision. The Church is the body of Christ, which has many members (Rom. 12:5). Each member has received gifts to use for the advancement of God's Kingdom (Rom. 12:6). Jesus gave seven gifts known as the motivational gifts: Prophecy, Ministry (Serving), Teaching, Giving, Exhortation (Encouraging), Leading, and Mercy (Rom. 12:6–8). These gifts are designed to serve God's Kingdom's agenda; they are called to serve human needs.

Servant leaders are those individuals who develop and empower others to reach their highest potential (Sendjaya and Sarros 2002). Servant Leadership embraces the notion that if the followers are maximizing their potential, this will directly translate into the realization of the potential of the organization, or, in other words, organizational performance (Gandolfi et al. 2017). Servant leaders encourage leaders and followers to raise one another to higher levels of motivation and morality. Servant Leadership, at the most fundamental level, works because it incorporates one of the proven elements of effective leadership in general. Effective leadership is not linear, nor is it a one-way form of communication or event; preferably, it is highly interactive (Northouse 2007). Servant Leadership is the most interactive style of leadership when it comes to leader/follower engagement, since the primary emphasis for attaining organizational goals is based on serving the followers who are tasked with achieving those goals.

Jesus' leadership was purpose-driven. His mission on earth was to promote God's Kingdom's agenda. Jesus desired for His followers to be good and faithful servants, committed to spreading the Kingdom's message throughout the world.

He blessed all His followers with gifts and abilities in order to produce a profit. They were to use their time, talents, and treasure to advance God's Kingdom. Jesus' relationship with God was the sole purpose of fulfilling His calling. He did not do anything without the acknowledgment of God. Jesus as the visionary moved with compassion to meet the needs of God's people. Jesus' vision was practical, solved problems, and was personal. It was designed to provide redemption, joy, hope, and love to the falling world. Jesus strategically positioned himself to launch God's Kingdom into the culture. He built a new community, trained His apprentices, mobilized His followers, modeled God's love, and took the risk for success. Jesus also taught His followers about Servant Leadership. They were called to develop and empower others to reach their highest potential (Sendjaya and Sarros 2002). Jesus' leadership provides a guide, inspiration, and support to His followers. His leadership maximized His followers' potential.

Chapter Seven

Leadership Styles

Courageous Christian Leadership requires leaders to have the faith to take risks, but these risks are calculated based on the organization's future. Courageous Christian Leaders must have a strategic approach to leadership. Their leadership styles must match their organizational strategies and structures in order to maximize organizational performance. The organization's design is determined in large part by the organizational environment (Burton et al. 2015). The organization must select the right leadership style in order to achieve organizational goals. Courageous Christian Leadership exhibits the leadership styles of a Transformational, Authentic, and Global Leader.

Becoming a courageous and impactful leader requires time and a commitment to the innovation process. An effective leader understands the organizational strategy, sets corporate direction, and supports workers. Becoming a great leader requires time, focus, and continuous effort:

> *To successfully lead through innovation and change, follow these guidelines: (a) Innovation leaders have a clear vision of what they want to accomplish and strong desire to make it happen. (b) Innovation leaders create successful experiences for the entire organization. Also, (c) Innovation leaders rethink how to refocus resources needed to respond to a new generation and global environment. (d) Innovation leaders introduce new ideas and concepts to educate and train professional and support staff. (e) Innovation leaders pursue organizational objectives instead of personal preferences.* (McCarthy 2015: 12)

INNOVATION PROCESS

Innovation is the process of developing and implementing new ideas. "It is about searching for ideas, exploring ideas, developing ideas, implementing ideas, and successfully introducing the ideas (products) into the marketplace" (Buijs 2007). The innovation process requires leadership to bridge the gap between dreams and reality, past and future, certainty and risk, the concrete and the abstract, us (we love innovation) and them (we don't want to change at all), and success and failure. Innovation leaders must be aware of inherent conflicts and inconsistent aspects of the innovation process. The innovation process is not like the daily business routine, which is repetitive, risk-avoidant, and predictable. To the contrary, innovation requires creativity, breaking the rules, risk taking, and challenging the organization to rise to the demands of the future. The innovation process creates oppositions within the organization. Innovation leaders are aware of these natural conflicts from daily routine processes within the firm. Dealing with these multiple aspects of innovation at the same time and harmonizing the different perspectives, views, and time horizons of the various team members and partner organizations call for a different type of leadership.

TRANSFORMATIONAL LEADERSHIP

Transformational Leadership is built upon seven factors, which have a profound effect on the relationship between leaders and followers. Transformational Leadership is contrasted with Transactional Leadership (two factors) and Laissez–Faire Leadership (one factor). Leaders can influence the motives of followers by helping them to reach the goals of the organization (Burns 1978). Leaders desire to fulfill the followers' needs and impact their lives for the collective good; they seek to raise the level of morality in followers in order to accomplish a goal. Transformational Leadership is socialized leadership that helps leaders transcend their interests for the sake of others and influence the ethics of the individuals (Northouse 2013). The leader emerges as the leader by position or service. However, Transformational Leaders seek to change and improve the personal, professional, and social lives of their followers. The leaders' primary responsibility is to make a difference within themselves, then nurture and cultivate the uniqueness of every follower. Leadership is not designed to be an island unto itself; its primary focus is to bring a group of individuals together to reach a common goal (Northouse 2013). Jesus, as a Change Agent, focused on building God's

Kingdom by promoting God's love for humanity and inspiring others to accept God's plan for salvation (John 3:16). In doing so, He recruited individuals to expand the gospel's message. The purpose of Transformational Leadership is to transform the individual's current situation or circumstance, change the group, organization, community, and eventually impact society. Transformational Leadership requires a leader who has character, courage, credibility, and charisma (Malphurs 2003). Charisma is a special gift that individuals possess; it gives them the capacity to do extraordinary things (Northouse 2013). A leader's ability to project strong characteristics and behaviors has a significant impact on followers.

TRANSFORMATIONAL LEADERSHIP MODEL

The Transformational Leadership model incorporates four factors. These four factors center on leaders' abilities to influence, inspire, stimulate, and consider their followers. No leaders are self-sufficient; they need others, and others need them. There is a reciprocal relationship between leaders and followers. A leader's capacity to influence creates a climate of change. Transformational Leaders desire to inspire followers to change and challenge them to grow morally. Transactional Leadership is different from Transformational Leadership, because it focuses on the exchange of value between the leader and the followers in order to advance both the leaders' and followers' agendas. Transactional Leaders are influential because it is in the best interest of the followers to do what their leaders want (Kuhnert and Lewis 1987). Lassiez–Faire Leadership is absent leadership, which takes a "hands-off" approach. This leader abandons responsibility, delays decisions, gives no feedback, and makes little effort to help followers satisfy their needs. There is no exchange with followers or attempt to help them grow (Northouse 2013).

Four Factors of Transformational Leadership

Transformational Leadership is built on four factors: idealized influence (charisma), inspirational motivation, intellectual stimulation, and individualized consideration.

Factor 1: Idealized influence is the emotional component of leadership; it involves the leaders being strong role models for followers; followers identify with the leaders and desire to imitate them. Transformational Leaders usually have very high standards of moral and ethical conduct and can be counted on to do the right thing (Northouse 2013).

Factor 2: Inspirational motivation is a quality of leaders who communicates high expectation to followers, inspiring them to be committed to and part of the shared vision (Northouse 2013). Kouzes and Posner (2012) note, "A leader inspires shared vision by envisioning the future; the imagination of exciting and ennobling possibilities and enlisting others in a common vision by appealing to shared aspiration" (p. 29). Rather than focusing on self-interest, a transactional leader inspires followers by using words of encouragement, symbols, and emotional appeals in order to focus group members' efforts to achieve team goals.

Factor 3: Intellectual stimulation occurs when the leaders inspire followers to be creative and innovative and to think outside of the usual parameter, by questioning their own beliefs and values, as well as those of the leader and the organization. Leaders that intellectually stimulate followers often support followers as they try to create new ideas or approaches to develop innovative ways of dealing with organizational issues. They encourage followers to think things out on their own and to engage in careful and creative problem solving.

Factor 4: Individual consideration provides leadership for the followers by creating a climate of listening carefully to followers' needs, with the leader acting as a coach or advisor, while trying to help followers grow personally, professionally, and socially (Northouse 2013: 29). Kouzes and Posner (2012) note that a Transformational Leader will "enable others to act, fostering collaboration by building trust and facilitating the relationship and strengthen others by increasing self-determination and developing competence" (p. 29). In this way, the leader's capacity to be supportive creates a collaborative climate.

AUTHENTIC LEADERSHIP

Leadership is a process, whereby an individual influences a group of individuals to achieve a common goal (Northouse 2013). Leaders are ethical role models; they have a moral responsibility to make the right decisions. Leaders should lead with care, justice, and critique (Ehrich et al. 2015), leading in a manner that boosts morale and stirs hope, treats people fairly, and also critiques and challenges the organization's power structure.

Leaders are obligated to make sound judgments when making decisions that impact the organization and followers. It is therefore essential for leaders to use a fundamental approach to making a decision. Leadership is about who you are (character); how you act (conduct); what you do (credibility); and how you work with others (collaboration) (Hackman and Johnson 2013). A leader must always apply the right decisions to gain the best results. Ethics gives leaders a road map or a playbook to follow in order to help them stay connected with followers. All leadership is value-laden, driven by ideas, and motivated by beliefs, which shows the leader's character (Ciulla 2014). Leadership ethics is a benefit for the organization and followers; it is the glue that holds the organization together. Followers prosper under effective leaders and suffer under ineffective leaders (Hackman and Johnson 2013). Ethics is the heart of leadership studies and has veins that run through all leadership research (Ciulla 2014). Leadership and ethics are essential for an organization's success.

What Is Ethics?

Ethics is an elusive word whose meaning can vary from one person to the next. It is very subjective. However, the field of ethics is typically divided into three branches: descriptive, prescriptive (normative), and metaethical (Fedler 2006). Descriptive ethics is not concerned with asking what people ought to do or how they should feel but focuses on how people actually behave, think, or feel regarding morality. Prescriptive or normative ethics suggests specific actions, behaviors, or modes of feeling. It seeks to establish norms (rules) for acting, thinking, and feeling. Metaethics is the investigation into how people use moral language and how they go about making ethical decisions. Ethics differs from, but is related to, morality. Morality is doing what is right. Ethics is born from and helps to carry out morality. It is an individual's beliefs, values, and practices. Ethics represents "fair dealing," which is essential to developing loyalty and trust in relationships and creates open communication (Ciulla 2014).

Christian Ethics

Christian ethics focuses on normative ethics: how to act, feel, or think, classified as decisionist ethics (how ought I do) and virtue ethics (how ought I be or live) (Fedler 2006). Christian ethics originates from the Jewish and Christian belief systems, where great emphasis is placed on living a life, not just of right belief, but of right action, disposition, and attitude. Christian leaders must strive to use ethics in their leadership practices. They must lead by faith to apply Christian virtues. The Apostle James said, "But someone will say, 'You have faith, and I have worked.' Show me your faith apart from your works, and I by my works will show you my faith" (James 2:18, NRSV). Leadership is action, not a position (McGannon 2012). Christian leaders are encouraged to use their faith to apply Christian virtues, which are faith, hope, and love (Wright 2010).

The Purpose of Leadership Ethics

God made a covenant with Abraham, who was considered the father of faith (Gen. 12:1–3). God promised Abraham protection, descendants, land, and blessings. He promised to bless him and his descendants if he obeyed His instructions. The Abrahamic covenant is an everlasting agreement. This agreement is one-sided because it is based on God's commitment to fulfill His promise. God promised to provide protection and blessings for the Hebrews. After many trials and setbacks, God revisited the Hebrews at Mount Sinai and established the Mosaic covenant. This agreement was predicated upon the Hebrews living according to God's plan. God established some conditions for how the Hebrews were to live.

God gave Moses a playbook to follow—613 instructions

for the Israelites to obey (Fedler 2006). God gave this code of ethics because He desired the Israelites to live differently from other nations. He chose Israel to be the model nation for other countries to follow, and through them "all the families of the earth" would be blessed (Gen. 12:3). God desired for Israel to represent His kingdom by being priests and a holy nation (Exodus 19:6). Other countries would see how God blessed Israel for obedience and punished them for disobedience (Deut. 28). God wanted Israel to model and manage His values.

The Apostle Paul encouraged believers to renew their minds, be transformed with God's word, and walk with a spirit of humility, because God has given everyone a measure of faith (Rom. 12:1–3). Christian leaders are encouraged to have a good testimony; they are to lead with character (virtue). Christian character should be guided by faith, hope, and love (Wright 2010). The Apostle Paul outlined these three virtues, along with nine variables, the fruit of the Spirit: love, joy, peace, longsuffering, kindness, goodness, faithfulness, gentleness, and self-control (Gal. 5:22). Christians are encouraged to live by faith, hope, and love, but if for some reason they get off track, the Holy Spirit is there to help them get back on track by applying the fruit of the Spirit.

Christian leaders lead with conviction; they are Authentic Leaders. Authentic Leaders are real and genuine. Their motives are pure; what you see is what you get. Authentic Leaders use their intrapersonal perspective to lead with conviction; they are not a copy, but an original (Northouse 2013). Authentic Leaders are empowered from interactions between leaders and followers; it is a reciprocal process. Both leaders and followers are affected because of the relationship; it is a mutual exchange that enriches their shared experience. Authentic Leaders are developed over a lifetime. Their leadership is nurtured from life experience and shaped by situations, circumstances, and trials. Christian leaders are encouraged to be examples and role models for their followers.

The Development of Authentic Leadership

Authentic Leaders build relationships with followers by being genuine, honest, and transparent. They seek an authentic relationship with their followers, which helps to foster trust, respect, and collaboration. Authentic Leadership is based on the genuineness of the leaders and their leadership. It is rooted in three continuums: intrapersonal perspective, interpersonal process, and developmental perspective. The Authentic Leader who has an intrapersonal perspective focuses on the leader and what is going on within the leader. The leader is leading from conviction, where the leadership is genuine and real, not copied or duplicated. Intrapersonal perspective emphasizes leaders' life experiences and their development from those personal experiences (Northouse 2013). The Authentic Leader who has an interpersonal process focuses on the relational capacity, which the leaders and followers create. Authentic Leaders initiate the leadership process by selecting, equipping, training, and influencing one or more individuals who may have diverse gifts, abilities, and skills. They also encourage followers to accept the organization's shared vision, values, and objectives, which inspire the followers to be willing and motivated to use passion, strength, and energy to achieve the organizational mission and goals (Winston and Patterson 2006). Authentic Leadership emerges from the interaction between leaders and followers, which is a reciprocal process, because the leader and the followers equally impact each other. Authentic Leaders have a developmental perspective, which can develop within a lifetime. They can be nurtured, rather than being born with fixed traits.

Global Leadership

Human beings are creatures of habit, and habits are sometimes hard to break. Leaders sometimes have the most difficult time while changing, because of past successes or failures. Finding new ways of doing things is challenging when the old ways work. Why fix something when it isn't broken? Global Leadership requires leaders to acquire a new mind-set and develop new skills. A Global Leader must think and act globally in order to transform a cross-cultural environment. Luke, the writer of the book of Acts, recalls the story of the Apostle Paul traveling through the city of Athens. Paul observed the artifacts and documents of the Athenian culture. He noticed an inscription on an altar that read: "To the unknown God." He then declared that he came representing the "unknown god" and that this God was Yahweh, revealed in Christ (Acts 17). He had to merge into the culture in order to understand the culture. Courageous Christian Leaders must also have the cultural agility to transform learning.

LEADERSHIP CULTURAL AGILITY

Cultural agility is the mega-competency that enables professionals to perform successfully in a cross-cultural situation. Cultural agility is a practice; building it is a process, not an event. Individuals develop cultural agility at different speeds, depending on their international career orientation, personality characteristics, language skills, and cross-cultural competencies. Leaders gain cultural agility by combining individual skills and abilities, motivation, and experience. There are three levels of cultural agility. Level one of cultural agility possesses the most critical cross-cultural competencies, where leaders possess the skills and abilities to have psychological ease, relate to others, and make effective decisions in a cross-cultural context (Caligiuri 2012). Level two of cultural agility uses cultural adaptation, cultural minimization, and cultural integration when needed and as appropriate. Level three assesses accurately and responds effectively in situations where the cultural context will affect the outcome. Leaders who possess cultural agility can read cross-cultural or multicultural situations, assess different behaviors, attitudes, and values, and respond successfully to the cross-cultural context.

Global Leaders are not born but made! Preparation for Global Leadership is necessary for an organization's success in a cross-cultural environment. Learning the right skills are crucial, but developing the right mind and heart is much more valuable. Leaders must possess the skills, personalities, and attitudes that will allow them to navigate the challenges of international business. Global Leaders must develop a global mind-set, global entrepreneurship, and global leadership. Global Leaders connect, create, and contribute to the cross-cultural environment.

Global Mind-Set

Global Leadership can connect with others in the cross-cultural environment. Global Leaders join with others by interpreting, analyzing, and decoding situations from a variety of perspectives in order to identify the best route to successful collaboration in a cross-cultural environment (Cabrera and Unruh 2012). A set of universally accepted behaviors in leadership are telling the truth, sharing valuable information with others, respecting others' property, keeping one's promises, and returning favors (Lawrence 2010). A leader develops a global mind-set by cultivating three forms of personal capital: global psychological capital (cognitive ability to analyze multiple points of view), global intellectual capital (ability to learn about each part of the world), and global social capital (social network expands into cross-cultural).

Global Entrepreneurship

Global Leaders' ability to act with a global mind-set works best when they create opportunities for others. They serve as global entrepreneurs who take advantage of their leverage because of a global mind-set that creates value (Cabrera and Unruh 2012). Global Leaders are both social and innovative, reaching across cultural boundaries in order to forge value-creating partnerships among businesses, governments, and society. Global entrepreneurship projects may be new start-ups or existing organizations; they may be social innovations or new products. Global entrepreneurs create values in many ways. Organizations and countries invite other groups to use their unique economic, political, and social advantage as leverage in the global marketplace (Guillen 2001).

Global Citizenship

Global Leaders are defined by how they contribute to improving their working environment. Global Leaders act as citizens of the world. They pursue challenges and opportunities in order to bring benefit to everyone involved. Global

Leaders do not exploit or take advantage of others by breaking the law but move according to a desire to make a positive contribution. Global Leaders are high-character individuals who play by the law of the land. (Khurana and Nohria 2008). Cultures are sometimes tough to decipher. Global Leaders possess the capacity to connect, create, and contribute value to the culture. They possess the mind-set and skills necessary to transform the cross-cultural environment. They have the mentality to analyze and decode and the background to properly evaluate cultural values. In this way, the leaders' focus shifts from self-interest to the world's needs. Cultural agility prepares the leaders for adaptation, minimization, and integration into the cross-cultural environment. Global Leaders are made, and not born, and they have a significant impact on the cross-cultural environment.

CONCLUSION

Organization innovation is essential for organizational success. Matching the right leadership with the challenge of change is critical. Transformational Leadership is the closest match to Courageous Christian Leadership because of the leader's intended purpose to inspire followers to reach beyond themselves, their self-ambition, and self-interest for the sake of advancing organizational goals. Transformational Leadership seeks to influence others in order to maximize their potential and inspire their creativity. Authentic Leaders are genuine leaders who lead by their convictions; they conduct their personal and professional lives with ethics. Ethics is essential to an organization's success; it is difficult for an organization to survive and thrive without ethics. Ethics is the playbook that helps the team win. Global Leaders possess the capacity to connect, create, and contribute value to the culture. Global Leaders possess the mind-set and skills necessary to transform the cross-cultural environment. They have the mentality necessary to analyze and decode the situation and to properly evaluate cultural values. The Global Leader's focus shifts from self-interest to the world's needs.

Chapter Eight

Courageous Leaders Passing the Leadership Baton

After the death of Moses, the servant of the Lord, God chose Joshua as the next Israelite leader. He charged Moses with the preparation of Joshua for leadership (Deut. 31:7-8, 14-16, 23). Moses passed the Leadership Baton to Joshua, who would take responsibility for leading the Israelites across the Jordan River (Deut. 31:1-6). Moses encouraged Joshua before the children of Israel,

> *Be strong and of good courage, for you must go with this people to the land which the Lord has sworn to their fathers to give them, and you shall cause them to inherit it. And the Lord, He is the one who goes before you. He*

will be with you; he will not leave you nor forsake you; do not fear nor be dismayed. (Deut. 31:7–8)

Furthermore, Moses empowered the Levites, those individuals who were responsible for the Ark of the Covenant of the Lord. He commanded them to place the Book of the Law besides the Ark of the Covenant (Deut. 31:24–26), where it would serve as a witness to the Israelites of how God expected the Israelites to govern themselves. Moses said to the Israelites,

> *Take this Book of the Law and put it beside the ark of the covenant of the Lord your God, that it may be there as a witness against you; for I know your rebellion and your stiff neck. If today, while I am yet alive with you, you have been rebellious against the Lord, then how much more after my death? Gather to me all the elders of your tribes, and your officers, that I may speak these words in their hearing and call heaven and earth to witness against them. I know that after my death you will become utterly corrupt and turn aside from the way which I have commanded you. And evil will befall you in the latter days because you will do evil in the sight of the Lord, to provoke Him to anger through the work of your hands.* (Deut. 31:26–29)

Moses passed the Leadership Baton to the Israelites' next generational leaders. They were expected to carry the leadership responsibilities so that the Israelites could successfully cross over the Jordan River. Moses passed on leadership authority to inspire those divinely entrusted with the task of serving God's purposes (Engstrom 1976).

> *A person can and will accept a communication as authoritative only when four conditions simultaneously obtain: (a) he can and does understand the communication; (b) at the time of his decision he believes that it is not*

inconsistent with the purpose of the organization; (c) at the time of his decision, he believes it to be compatible with his personal interest as a whole; and (d) he is able mentally and physically to comply with it. (Engstrom and Mackenzie 1974)

Joshua's authority to lead came from God through Moses (Josh. 1:1–9). God gave Joshua a spiritual authority to lead the Israelites. Spiritual authority is the power to support the opening of the entire universe and especially of the life of human beings toward union with the ultimate redeeming reality (Baier 2010). However, spiritual power is not private property; it is only real insofar as it is passed on to others. According to Baier,

Christian tradition knows several holders of this power: God, Jesus Christ, the angels, the saints and priests, spiritual guides, and finally each Christian and person of goodwill. They all are spiritual authorities and together create a field of liberating power with many interdependent centers. One can conceive of spiritual authority in Christianity as a complex interplay between these various forces. The manifestation of spiritual power through them does not take place for its own sake, or to celebrate the holder of the spiritual authority, but to empower other centers. In the field of human spiritual authority, tensions and struggles arise if the flow of authority is blocked by a center attempting to monopolize spiritual power for the establishment of an illusionary self-identity. (p. 107)

Joshua passed the Leadership Baton to the Israelite officers. They were given the spiritual authority to lead the Israelites under the influence of Joshua (Josh.1:10–18). At the end of his life, Joshua encouraged the next generation of leaders to continue to serve God.

"Now, therefore, fear the Lord, serve Him in sincerity and truth, and put away the gods which your fathers served on the other side of the River and in Egypt. Serve the Lord! And if it seems evil to you to serve the Lord, choose for yourselves this day whom you will serve, whether the gods which your fathers served that were on the other side of the River or the gods of the Amorites, in whose land you dwell. But as for me and my house, we will serve the Lord. So, the people answered and said: Far be it from us that we should forsake the Lord to serve other gods" (Josh. 24:14–16).

All spiritual authority comes from God, who desires that all humans experience His love. Now, the Courageous Christian Leaders must spread the Kingdom message of faith, hope, and love (1 Cor. 13:13). They must serve God faithfully by encouraging, enriching, and empowering the next generation to reach the world for Christ.

EMPOWERING THE NEXT-GENERATION LEADERS

Humanity is God's greatest creation on earth. He created humans in His image according to His will (Gen. 1:27). Humans were created on purpose and for a purpose. Adam, the first human, worked in the Garden of Eden (Gen. 2:15). Witherington (2011) notes that work, from a biblical point of view, involves a calling—a vocation—and, if done right, a ministry (p. 12). Christian Leaders have a responsibility to lead God's people. The Apostle Peter encouraged the elders to shepherd the flock of God by exercising oversight. A leader must be a faithful steward of God's greatest resources: people.

Jesus inspired steady leadership. He wanted His disciples

to lead differently from others. He encouraged Servant Leadership. Jesus' passion for doing the Father's work was paramount; His mission to complete God's work was His food (John 4:34). Christian Leaders must take the same attitude. They are responsible for being faithful; they must handle God's most significant asset (humans) with care. Jesus shared the story of a master who gave his three servants gifts according to their abilities. He gave one five talents, another two talents, and the last servant one talent (Matt. 25:15–30). The servants were each responsible for their assignment; they were each called to produce. Now, the one with five talents produced five more talents. The master said to him, "Well done good and faithful servant, you've been faithful over little, I will set you over much, enter into the joy of your master" (Matt. 25:21).

Next, the servant who received two talents brought back two more talents. The master complimented this servant in the same manner as the first servant, "Well done good and faithful, you've been faithful over little, I will set you over much, enter into the joy of your master" (Matt. 25:21). Finally, the last servant stepped forward with the one talent that he had received; the master was upset and disappointed because this servant was faithless, irresponsible, and failed to follow his master's order to produce. The master called him a wicked and lazy servant and cast him away from his presence (Matt. 25:24–28). Jesus expects Christian Leaders to be good and faithful servants who manage God's resources well. Christian Leaders must lead the people from a sincere heart, not for personal gain, advancements, or rewards, but only with a willing attitude.

Christian Leaders are called to set examples for their followers. The Apostle Paul commanded Timothy, his son in the faith, to set before the believers an example in speech, in conduct, in love, in faith, and in purity (I Tim. 4:11). Leaders are an organization's ambassadors of shared values (Kouzes and Posner 2012). Therefore, in order to effectively manage people, the leaders model the behavior they wish to inspire. They must clarify values by finding their voice and affirming shared values that they want to see in their followers, mentoring their followers to pursue shared organizational values, and setting examples that align with the organization (pp. 29–30). Leadership is a relationship that leaders use to mobilize others to want to struggle for shared aspirations. Christian Leaders must follow Christ's example and inspire followers to support them.

Leaders Empower Followers through Mentoring and Coaching

Jesus trained His disciples in personal-learning environments. He called His disciples together and taught about God's kingdom in the parable (Mark 12:1–11). He also trained His disciples in servanthood (John 13:1–17). He provided personal learning for His disciples' personal development. Personal learning is acquired knowledge, skills, or competencies that lead to the growth and development of an individual's interpersonal competencies (Lankau and Scandura 2002). Personal learning comprises individuals' understanding of their strengths and weaknesses, identity awareness and values, and individual developmental needs, reactions, and behavioral patterns (Kram 1996; Higgins and Kram 2001). By actively working with others, the individuals learn because the working environment helps develop the individual skills through continuous learning experiences that span multiple positions and numerous possible organizations (Liu and Fu 2011). Individuals with elevated levels of personal learning can continuously learn from others regardless of their rank or position (Lankau and Scandura 2007).

Organization's Culture for Personal Learning

Personal learning is divided into two dimensions: relational and personal skill development (Lankau and Scandura 2002). Relational learning is learning in the context of how an individual's work is related to the work of others (Bradford et al. 2017). However, personal learning is the development of personal skills that make for a better working environment. Individuals develop personal skills by interacting with others, listening actively, and solving problems in social contexts. Training is the systematic acquisition of knowledge, skills, and abilities in order to improve work performance (Grossman and Salas 2011). Organizations work to offer programs that lead to a higher degree of competence and enhance work performance.

Organizations today are moving toward a specific training platform (Cron et al. 2005). In particular, the emergence of networking technology has changed how information can be shared and how knowledge can be delivered (Tanner et al. 2005). In other words, the traditional methods of delivery, such as classroom lectures and training seminars, are being replaced with more high-tech instructional designs. Classroom simulations and remote learning modules are the norms for training (Zhang et al. 2004).

PASSING THE LEADERSHIP BATON THROUGH MENTORING AND COACHING

Organizational leaders must create learning cultures that use mentoring and coaching to develop followers. Most argue that mentoring and coaching are different from one another. A mentor may be a coach, but a coach is not necessarily a mentor (Moen and Allgood 2009; Parsloe and Wray 2001). Mentoring is the interpersonal exchange between a senior-experienced person (mentor) and a less-experienced junior person (protégé). The mentor provides support, direction, and feedback regarding career plans and personal development (Haggard et al. 2011).

Mentoring Is Essential to the Protégé and Organizational Success

A mentor is someone who has expertise in an area and is willing to share that information and experience with someone (a protégé) who has less experience. Mentoring relationships are essential to increase academic success regardless of professional focus (Holmes et al. 2007). Mentoring helps establish and strengthen the relationship between mentor and protégé, which is built on trust and respect and creating a collaborative culture. Mentors may serve as coaches, role models, brokers, and advocates (Stone 2007). The mentor approaches the mentoring process as helping the protégé with his or her current position and career. The mentoring process goes above and beyond coaching; it's a relationship that does more than train workers to do their jobs better; instead, it strives to share wisdom and experience in order to enable the protégé to take on responsibilities beyond his or her designated job description.

Mentoring has an expedited learning curve that places the worker on the fast track to higher performance and increases communication of organizational values and the creation of an innovative environment. The Apostle Paul inspired the church at Corinth to follow him. He said, "Be imitators of me, as I am of Christ" (1 Cor. 11:1).

Coaching Is Valuable to Increase the Protégé's Working Performance

A coach is someone from outside the organization who is compensated for helping to improve the performance of individuals within the organization (Judge and Cowell 1997). Initially, the field of coaching was conceived as a means of saving a derailed manager, and the coach was brought in after a crisis to help rehabilitate the manager. However, now the coach intervenes before the manager's situation becomes a crisis. Currently, coaching tends to occur much earlier, like the personal trainers hired by athletes to improve their performances. A world-record sprinter might employ a trainer to help improve his or her performance, even though the sprinter is a superior performer (Judge and Cowell 1997). When people are coached, they can increase performance in their current role and have the potential to do more in the future (Stone 2007). Coaching internally or externally can identify individuals' strengths and weakness, set goals, and discover answers to operational problems. Leaders who master the skill of coaching can boost their workers' performance by instructing them on what to do and how to do it most effectively, positively reinforcing good work, and finding ways to redesign responsibilities and increase workers' efforts.

The Difference between the Mentoring and the Coaching Process

The mentoring process involves frequent interaction between the mentor and the protégé in order to enhance the protégé's competencies and aid his or her career advancement (Haggard et al. 2011). Coaching is a process of improving performance by focusing on correcting problems with the work being done (Fournies 1987). Some scholars believe coaching is a process of empowering others to exceed established performance levels (Burdett 1998). Coaching refers to the coach teaching the coachee about organizational practices, rules, and politics (Richardson 2009). Despite the dissimilarities between coaching and mentoring, the general sentiment is that mentoring is relational and involves the developmental relationship between mentor and protégé (Braford et al. 2017). Coaching, on the other hand, is functional and exists due to the organizational need to maintain performance standards. Leaders are expected to coach their followers as a requirement of their tasks (Richardson 2009). Coaching helps the learner personalize the teaching material and to make the connection from theory to practice, from abstract examples and study material to real-world challenges the learner might face (Hill et al. 1989).

Joshua was selected as the Next-Generation Leader who moved the Israelites across the Jordan River. Joshua, the spiritual leader, had the spiritual authority to encourage, enrich, and empower the leaders to follow God's plan. Joshua managed the Israelites' progress in order to make sure they obeyed God's instructions. He passed the Leadership Baton to the officers of the tribes, and they took on the responsibility for carrying on that spiritual authority. These Courageous Leaders defeated the seven nations in the land of Canaan (Josh. 3:9–10).

There will always be a strong need for Courageous Christian Leadership. Eighty-four percent of organizations anticipate a shortfall in leaders in the next five years (Tuck n.d.). Passing the Leadership Baton requires organizations to empower the next generation of leaders to move the organization into a global environment. Leaders must create a personal learning environment in which protégés are mentored and coached in order to reach greater performance. Mentoring and coaching cultivate a collaborative working environment, where useful feedback is welcome.

Summary

The world is changing rapidly with globalization. Globalization impacts technology, transportation, and communication. These changes create a desperate need for leadership that is future-smart. The leaders of tomorrow must be problem solvers, socially intelligent, and adaptive in order to impact their environments. Courageous Christian Leadership is prepared to empower the Next Generation of Leaders. They are aware of their strengths, weaknesses, threats, and opportunities. Leadership is not for the weak at heart. Instead, Courageous Christian Leaders lead on purpose. God's spiritual authority guides them. These leaders are purpose-driven, influential, visionary, pragmatic, and ethical. They prepare their organizations to move into the future. God desires the world to be transformed by the influence of God's Kingdom (Matt. 6:1–10). The leader is a change agent with the mission to "Change the World for Christ." Courageous Christian Leaders apply the leadership styles of Transformational, Authentic, and Global Leadership in order to impact organizational cultures. They pass the Leadership Baton to the Next Generation of Leaders through the processes of mentoring and coaching. They create a collaborative culture for personal learning so that their organizations are ready to meet the high demand for credible and qualified leadership.

Summary

References

Agnieszka Tennant. 2005. "The making of the Christian: Richard J. Foster and Dallas Willard on the difference between discipleship and Christian formation." *Christianity Today* 49(10):42.

Alimo-Metcalfe, B., and J. Alban-Metcalfe. 2001. "The construction of a new transformational leadership questionnaire." *Journal of Occupational & Organizational Psychology* 79:1–27.

Alban-Metcalfe, J., & Alimo-Metcalfe, B. 2007. Development of a private sector version of the (Engaging) Transformational Leadership Questionnaire. *Leadership & Organization Development Journal,* 28(2), 104-121.

Allen, D., and E. O. Springsted. 2007. *Philosophy for Understanding Theology.* Louisville: Westminster John Knox Press.

Ames, R. 2003. Confucianism and Deweyian pragmatism: a dialogue. *Journal of Chinese Philosophy* 30(3–4): 403–417.

Amnesty International. 2004. War on Global Values. http://www. globalissues.org/article/138/hu:man-rights-for-all.

Anderson, A. 2001. *African Reformation: African Initiated Christianity in the 20th Century.* Trenton: Africa World Press, Inc.

Ashford, S. J., and J. Detert. 2015. The boss to buy in. *Harvard Business Review.* www.hbr.org.

Ault, N. J. 2013. Theological reflection and spiritual direction. *The Australasian Catholic Record* 90(1):81–91. http://dx.doi.org/http:// eres.regent.edu:2048/ login?url=https://search-proquestcom.ezproxy. regent.edu /docview/1345943354?accountid=13479.

Baer, L. L., A. H. Duin, and D. Bushway. 2015. Change agent leadership. *Planning for Higher Education* 43(3):1–11. http://dx.doi.org/ http://eres.regent.edu:2048/login?url=https://search-proquest-com. ezproxy.regent.edu/docview/1706580348?accountid=13479.

Baier, K. 2010. Spiritual authority: a Christian perspective. *University of Hawai'i Press* 30:109–117.

Barrett, R. 1998. *Liberating the Corporate Soul: Building a Visionary Organization.* Boston: Butterworth-Heinemann.

Bazerman, M. H., and A. E. Tenbrunsel. 2011. *Blind Spots: Why We Fail to do What's Right and What to do about It.* Princeton: Princeton University Press.

Beale. 2004. *The Temple and the Church's Mission.* Downers Grove: Intervarsity Press.

Birmingham, M., and W. J. Connolly. 1994. *Witnessing to the Fire: Spiritual Direction and the Development of Directors, One Center's Experience.* Kansas City: Sheed & Ward.

Bloesch, D. 2007. *Spirituality Old and New: Recovering Authentic Spiritual Life.* Downers Grove: IVP Academic.

Borg, M. J. 1987. *Jesus a New Vision.* San Francisco: Harper & Row.

Bower, J. L. 1970. *Managing the Resource Allocation Process.* Boston: Harvard Business School.

Bradford, S. K., B. N. Rutherford, and S. B. Friend. 2017. The impact of training, mentoring and coaching on personal learning in the sales environment. *International Journal of Evidence Based Coaching & Mentoring* 15(1):133–151. http://dx.doi.org/http:// eres.regent.edu:2048/login?url=http://search.ebscohost.com/login. aspx?direct=true&db=bth&AN=123711264&site=ehost-live.

Buckley, M. J. 1989. "Seventeenth-Century French Spirituality: Three Figures." *In Christian Spirituality: Post-Reformation and Modern,* edited by L. Dupre, D. E. Saliers, and J. Meyendorff, 28–68.

Buijs, J. 2007. Innovation Leaders should be controlled Schizophrenics. *Creativity and Innovation Management* 16(2):203–210.

Burdett, J. 1998. Forty things every manager should know about coaching. *Journal of Management Development* 17(2):142–152.

Burgelman, R. A. 1983. A model of the interaction of strategic behaviors, corporate, context, and the concept of strategy. *Academy of Management Review* 8:61–70.

Burgelman, R. A. 1991. Intraorganizational ecology of strategy making and organizational adaptation: theory and field research. *Organization Science* 2, 239–262.

Burgelman, R. A. 1994. Fading memories: a process theory of strategic business exit in dynamic environments. *Administrative Science Quarterly* 39:24–57.

Burke, T. J. 2012. Paul's new family in Thessalonica. *Novum Testamentum* 54(3):269–287. http://dx.doi.org/10.1163/156853612X632471.

Burns, J. M. 1978. *Leadership.* New York: Harper & Row.

Burton, R. M., B. Obel, and D. D. Hakonsson. 2015. *Organizational Design: A Step-by-Step Approach.* 3rd ed. Cambridge: University Printing House.

Cabrera, A., and G. Unruh. 2012. *Being Global: How to Think, Act, and Lead in a Transformed World.* Boston: Harvard Business Review Press.

Caligiuri, P. 2012. *Cultural Agility: Building a Pipeline of Successful Global Professionals*. San Francisco: Jossey-Bass.

Canton, J. 2015. *Future Smart*. Boston: Da Capo Press.

Caraman, P. 1990. *Ignatius Loyola: A Biography of the Founder of the Jesuits*. San Francisco: Harper & Row, Publishers.

Chan, S. 1999. *Spiritual Theology: A Systematic Study of the Christian Life*. Downers Grove: InterVarsity Press.

Cheung, S., P. Wong, and A. Wu. 2011. Towards an organizational culture framework in construction. *International Journal of Project Management* 29(1):33–44. http://dx.doi.org/https://doi.org/10.1016/j.ijproman.2010.01.014.

Chidester, D. 1996. *Savage Systems: Colonialism and Comparative Religion in Southern Africa*. Charlottesville: University Press of Virginia.

Ciulla, J. B. 2014. *Ethics, the Heart of Leadership*. Santa Barbara: Praeger.

Clarke, A. D. 2008. *A Pauline Theology of Church Leadership*. London: Bloomsbury.

Cole, N. 2005. *Organic Church: Growing Faith where Life Happens*. San Francisco: Jossey-Bass.

Cole, N. 2010. *Church 3.0*. San Francisco: Jossey-Bass.

Collins, J. C., and J. I. Porras. 1994. *Built to Last: Successful Habits of Visionary Companies*. New York: The Free Press/Harper Business.

Conger, J. A. 1999. Charismatic and transformational leadership in organizations: an insider's perspective on these developing streams of research. *Leadership Quarterly* 10(2):145–179.

Consideration. 2015. In *Merriam-Webster Online*. http://dx.doi.
org/http://www.merriam-webster.com.ezproxy.regent.edu:2048/
dictionary/consideration.

Corbin, C. 2000. *Great Leaders See the Future First: Taking Your
Organization to the Top in Five Revolutionary Steps*. http://dx.doi.org/
http://eres.regent.edu:2048/login?url=http://search.ebscohost.com/
login.aspx? direct=true&db=nlebk&AN=38900&sAite=ehost-live.

Creyton, M. 2014. Adaptive leadership: an approach
for challenging times. *Volunteering Queensland*. http://
dx.doi.org/www.voiunteeringqld.org.au/docs/innovate
_Research_Bulletin_Adaptive_Leadership_an_App.

Cron, W., G. Marshall, J. Singh, R. Spiro, and H. Sujan. 2005.
Salesperson selection, training, and development: trends, implica-
tions, and research opportunities. *Journal of Personal Selling and Sales
Management* 25(2):124–136.

Cullen, K. L., B. D. Edwards, W. C. Casper, and K. R. Gue. 2013.
Employees' adaptability and perceptions of change-related uncertainty: implications for perceived organizational support, job satisfac-
tion, and performance. *Journal of Business* 29:1–12.

Currie, T. I. 2006. 1 Thessalonians 5:12-24. *Interpretation*
60(4):446–449.

Dale, R. 2006. Leading Edge: *Leadership Strategies from the New
Testament*. Wipf and Stock Publishers.

Davies, B. n.d. Acting strategically and taking strategic. Retrieved
January 25, 2019. http://www.leadershipsolutions.co.za/strategic-act-
ing-cont1.html.

Deal, T. E., and A. A. Kennedy. 1982. *Corporate Cultures*. New York:
Perseus.

Deal, T. E., and A. A. Kennedy. 1999. *The New Corporate Cultures*. New York: Perseus.

Demarest, B. 2001. *Satisfy Your Soul: Restoring the Heart of Christian spirituality*. Colorado Springs: Nave Press.

DeYoung, R. K. 2013. Courage as a Christian virtue. *Journal of Spiritual Formation & Soul Care* 6(2):301–312. http://dx.doi.org/http://eres.regent.edu:2048/login?url=http://search.ebscohost.com/login.aspx?direct=true&db=rfh&AN=ATLA0001967426&site=ehost-live.

Duncan, E. A., and G. L. Warden. 1999. Influential leadership and change environment: the role leaders play in the growth and development of the people they lead. *Journal of Healthcare Management* 44(4):225–226. http://dx.doi.org/http://eres.regent.edu:2048/login?url=https://search-proquest-com.ezproxy.regent.edu/docview/206732525?accountid=13479.

Edmonstone, J., and J. Western. 2002. Leadership development in health care: what do we know? *Journal of Health Organization and Management* 16(1):34–47.

Edwards, D. 1983. *Human Experience of God*. New York: Paulist Press.

Ehrich, L. C., J. Harris, V. Klenowski, J. Smeed, and N. Spina. 2015. The centrality of ethical leadership. *Journal of Educational Administration* 53(2):197–214.

Emiliani, M. L. 2008. Standardized work for executive leadership. *Leadership & Organization Development Journal* 29(1):24–46. http://dx.doi.org/http://dx.doi.org.ezproxy .regent.edu:2048/10.1108/014377 30810845289.

Englund, H. 2003. Christian independency and global membership: Pentecostal extraversions in Malawi. *Journal of Religion in Africa* 33:83–111.

Engstrom, T. W. 1976. *The Making of a Christian Leader*. Grand Rapids: Zondervan.

Engstrom, T. W., and R. A. Mackenzie. 1974. *Managing Your Time*. Grand Rapids: Zondervan Publishing House.

Evans, J. 2015. Experience and convergence in spiritual direction. *Journal of Religion and Health* 54(1):264–278. http://dx.doi.org/http://dx.doi.org.ezproxy.regent.edu:2048/10.1007/s10943-014-9824-4.

Fedler, K. 2006. *Exploring Christian Ethics: Biblical Foundations for Morality*. Louisville: Westminster John Knox Press.

Floyd, S. W., and B. Wooldridge. 1997. Middle management's strategic influence and organizational performance. *Journal of Management Studies* 34:3.

Flyvbjerg, B. 2001. *Making Social Science Matter: Why Social Inquiry Fails and How It Can Succeed Again*. Cambridge: Cambridge University Press.

Ford, L. 1991. *Transforming Leadership*. Downers Grove: Intervarsity Press.

Fournies, F. 1987. *Coaching for Improved Work Performance*. New York: Liberty Hall Press.

Fullenbach, J. 2002. *Church: Community for the Kingdom*. Maryknoll: Orbis Books.

Gandolfi, F., S. Stone, and F. Deno. 2017. Servant leadership: an ancient style with 21st century relevance. *Revista De Management Comparat International* 18(4):350–361. http://dx.doi.org/http://eres.regent.edu:2048/login?url=https://search-proquest-com.ezproxy.regent.edu/docview/2011218218?accountid=13479.

Gavetti, G. 2011. The new psychology of strategic leadership.

Harvard Business Review. http://dx.doi.org/https://hbr.org/2011/07/the-new-psychology-of-strategic-leadership.

Geertz, C. 1973. *The Interpretation of Cultures.* New York: Basic Books.

Gleeson, B. 2016. The mission of the Kingdom of God: ultimate source of meaning, value, and energy for Jesus. *The Australasian Catholic Record* 93(3):326–339.

Goffman, E. 1959. *The Presentation of Self in Every Day Life.* New York: Doubleday.

Goffman, E. 1967. *Interaction Ritual.* New York: Aldine.

Goldman, G. M. 2010. Church: seeking first the Kingdom of God. *Compass* 44(2):3–9. http://dx.doi.org/http://eres.regent.edu:2048/login?url=https://search-proquest-com.ezproxy.regent.edu/docview/853647049?accountid=13479.

Goldsmith, M. 2006. Are leaders acting on their training? *Strategic HR Review* 3:3. http://dx.doi.org/http://eres.regent.edu:2048/login?url=https: //search-proquest-com.ezproxy.regent.edu/docview/217171347?accountid=13479.

Gordon, G. G. and N. DiTomaso. 1992. Predicting corporate performance from organizational culture. *Journal of Management Studies* 29(6):783–798.

Greenleaf, R. K. 1977. *Servant Leadership: A Journey into the Nature of Legitimate Power and Greatness.* New York: Paulist Press.

Grossman, R., and E. Salas. 2011. The transfer of training: what really matters. *International Journal of Training and Development* 15(2):103–120.

Guardini, R. 1962. The phenomenology of religious experience. *Philosophy Today* 6:88–92.

Gudykunst, W. B., and S. Ting-Toomey. 1988. *Culture Interpersonal Communication.* Newbury Parks: Sage.

Guillen, M. F. 2001. *The Limits of Convergence.* Princeton: Princeton University Press.

Hackman, M. Z., and C. E. Johnson. 2013. *Leadership: A Communication Perspective.* 6th ed. Long Grove: Waveland Press, Inc.

Haggard, D., T. Dougherty, D. Turban, and J. Wilbanks. 2011. Who is a mentor? A review of evolving definitions and implications for research. *Journal of Management* 37(1):280–304.

Harvie, T. 2009. *Jürgen Moltmann's Ethics of Hope: Eschatological Possibilities for Moral Action.* Ashgate: Surrey.

Hatch, M. 2013. *Organization Theory: Modern, Symbolic and Postmodern Perspectives.* 3rd ed. Oxford: Oxford University Press.

Hatch, M. J., and M. Schultz. 2004. *Organizational Identity: A Reader.* Oxford: Oxford University Press.

Heath, C., and D. Heath. 2010. *Switch: How to Change Things When Change Is Hard.* New York: Crown Publishing Group.

Heifetz, R., A. Grashow, and M. Linsky. 2009. *The Practice of Adaptive Leadership: Tools and Tactics for Changing Your Organization and the World.* Boston: Harvard Business School Publishing.

Hemphill, J. K. 1949. *Situational Factors in Leadership.* Columbus: Ohio State University Bureau, Bureau of Educational Research.

Hesselbein, F., Goldsmith, M., and Leader to Leader Institute. 2006. *The Leader of the Future 2: Visions, Strategies, and Practices for the New Era.* 1st ed. http://dx.doi.org/http://eres. regent.edu:2048 /login?url=http://search.ebscohost.com/login. aspx?direct=true&db=e000xna&AN=170549&site=ehost-live.

Higgins, M., and K. Kram. 2001. Reconceptualizing mentoring at work: a developmental network perspective. *Academy of Management Review* 26(2):264–288.

Hill, S. K., M. H. Bahniuk, J. Dobos, and D. Rouner. 1989. Mentoring and other communication support in the academic setting. *Group & Organization Management* 14(3):355–368.

Holdcroft, B. B. 2006. What is religiosity? *Catholic Education: A Journal of Inquiry and Practice* 10(1):88–103.

Hollander, E. P. 2009. *Inclusive Leadership: The Essential Leader-Follower Relationship.* New York: Routledge/Psychology Press/Taylor & Francis.

Holmes, S., L. Land, and V. Hinton-Hudson. 2007. Race still matters: considerations for mentoring black women in academe. *The Negro Educational Review* 58(1–2):105–129.

Horwath, R. 2008. Strategy's most frequently asked questions. *Strategic Thinker.* http://dx.doi.org/http://strategyskills.com/Articles_Samples/ST-Strategys_FAQs.pdf.

Houston, J. M. 2008. Seeking historical perspectives for spiritual direction and soul care today. *Journal of Spiritual Formation & Soul Care* 1(1):88–105.

How to enhance strategic thinking: the role of competency models. 2016. https://doi-org.ezproxy.regent.edu/10.1108/HRMID-07-2016-0112.

Hughes, R. L., K. C. Beatty, and D. L. Dinwoodie. 2014. *Become a Strategic Leader.* 2nd ed. San Francisco: Jossey-Bass.

Hultman, K. 2002. *Balancing Individual and Organizational Values. Walking the Tightrope to Success.* San Francisco: Jossey-Bass/Pfeiffer.

Hunt, J. G. 1999. Transformational/charismatic leadership's transformation of the field: an historical essay. *Leadership Quarterly* 10(2):129–144.

Iacocca, L., and W. Novak. 1984. *Iacocca: An Autobiography.* New York: Bantam.

Isichei, E. 2004. *The Religious Traditions of Africa: A History.* Westport: Praeger.

Ivens, M. 1998. SJ. *Understanding the Spiritual Exercises.* Trowbridge: Cromwell Press.

Jenkins, P. 2006. *The New Faces of Christianity: Believing the Bible in the Global South.* Boston: Oxford University Press.

Johnson, B. L., and R. D. Moore. 2017. Soul care for one and all: Pentecostal theology and the search for a more expansive view of spiritual formation. *Journal of Pentecostal Theology* 26(1):125–152. http://dx.doi.org/https://doi-org.ezproxy.regent. edu/10.1163/17455251-02601010.

Jones, M. O., M. D. Moore, and R. C. Snyder. 1988. *Inside Organizations.* Newbury Park: Sage.

Judge, W. Q., and J. Cowell. 1997. The brave new world of executive coaching. *Business Horizons* 40(7):71–77. http://dx.doi.org/https://doi. org/10.1016/S0007-6813(97)90042-2.

Karkkainen, V. M. 2002. *An Introduction to Ecclesiology.* Downer Grover: Intervarsity Press.

Kaugman, R. C. 2009. Becoming your own leader: from leader to possible failure and back again—a pragmatic approach. *Performance Improvement* 48(4):29–34. http://dx.doi.org/http://eres.regent. edu:2048/login?url=https://search-proquest-com.ezproxy.regent.edu/ docview/237242617?accountid=13479.

Khurana, R., and N. Nohria. 2008. It's time to make management a true profession. *Harvard Business Review* 86, no. 10: 70-77.

Kihlstrom, J. F., and N. Cantor. 2000. "Social Intelligence." In *Handbook of Intelligence.* 2nd ed., edited by R. J. Sternberg. Cambridge: Cambridge University Press.

Klagge, J. 1996. Defining, discovering and developing personal leadership in organizations. *Leadership & Organization Development Journal* 17(5):38–45. http://dx.doi.org/http://eres.regent.edu:2048/login?url=https://search-proquest-com.ezproxy.regent.edu/docview/226913577?accountid=13479.

Knights, D. O., and M. O'Leary 2006. Leadership, ethics, and responsibility to the other. *Journal of Business Ethics* 67(2):125–137.

Kouzes, J., and B. Posner. 2012. *The Leadership Challenge: How to Make Extraordinary Things Happen in Organizations.* 5th ed. San Francisco: The Leadership Challenge.

Kram, K. 1996. "A Relational Approach to Career Development." In *The CareerIs Dead—Long Live the Career,* edited by D. Hall and Associates. San Francisco: Jossey Bass.

Kuhnert, K. W., and P. Lewis. 1987. Transactional and transformational leadership: a constructive/development analysis. *Academy of Management Review* 12(4):648–657.

Lankau, M., and T. Scandura. 2002. An investigation of personal learning in mentoring relationships: Content, antecedents, and consequences. *Academy of Management Journal* 45(1):779–790.

Lankau, M., and T. Scandura. 2007. "Mentoring as a Forum for Personal Learning in Organizations." In *The Handbook of Mentoring at Work: Theory, Research and Practice,* 95–122.

Lawrence, P. 2010. *Driven to Lead: Good, Bad and Misguided Leadership.* San Francisco: Jossey-Bass.

Leavy, B. 2015. Bill George: the era of self-serving leadership is over but global markets pose the next authenticity challenge for leaders. *Strategy & Leadership* 43(6):25–32. http://0search.proquest.com. library.regent.edu/docview/ 1734101353accountid=1347.

Lemler, J. B. 2010. Identity and effectiveness in the twenty-first century. *Anglican Theological Review* 92(1):89–102. http://dx.doi.org/ http://eres.regent.edu:2048/ login?url=https://search-proques com. ezproxy.regent.edu/docview /215261534?accountid=13479.

Liu, D., and P. Fu. 2011. Motivating protégés' personal learning in teams: a multilevel investigation of autonomy support and autonomy orientation. *Journal of Applied Psychology* 96(6):1195–1208.

Lockwood, G. J. 2009. The house church: from acts to Constantine. *Lutheran Theological Journal* 43(2):97–100. http://dx.doi.org/http:// eres.regent.edu:2048/login?url=https://search-proquest-com.ezproxy. regent.edu/docview/213743601?accountid=13479.

Lord, R. G., D. J. Brown, J. L. Harvey, and R. J. Hall. 2001. Contextual constraints on prototype generation and their multilevel consequences for leadership perceptions. *Leadership Quarterly* 12(3):311–338.

MacMullen, R. 2014. Religious toleration around the year 313. *Journal of Early Christian Studies* 22(4):499–517. http://dx.doi.org/http:// eres.regent.edu:2048/login?url=https://search-proquest-com.ezproxy. regent.edu/docview/1640568041?accountid=13479.

Magesa, L. 2004. *Anatomy of Inculturation: Transforming the Church in Africa.* Maryknoll: Orbis Books.

Malphurs, A. 2003. *Being Leaders.* Grand Rapids: Baker Books.

Manglos, N. 2011. Brokerage in the sacred sphere: religious leaders as community problem solvers in rural Malawi. *Sociological Forum* 26(2):334–355. http://dx.doi.org/ https://doi-org.ezproxy.regent. edu/10.1111/j.1573-7861.2011.01243.x.

Manuele, F. A. 2015. Culture change agent. *Professional Safety* 60(12):38–44. http://dx.doi.org/http://eres.regent.edu:2048/ login?url=https://search-proquest-com.ezproxy.regent.edu/ docview/1744735878?accountid=13479.

Marquis, B. L., and C. J. Huston. 2009. *Leadership Roles and Management Functions in Nursing.* 6th ed. Philadelphia: Lippincott Williams & Wilkins.

Martin, A. 2012. For social media buy-in, lead with the "why". *Harvard Business Review.* http://www.hbr.org.

Matthews, B. W., and T. Crocker. 2016. Defining "buy-in": introducing the buy-in continuum. *Organization Development Journal* 34(2):81–96. http://dx.doi.org/http://eres.regent.edu:2048/ login?url=https://search-proquest-com.ezproxy.regent.edu/ docview/1791020588?accountid=13479.

May, G. 1992. *Care of Mind, Care of Spirit: A Psychiatrist Explores Spiritual Direction.* New York: Harper Collins.

McCarthy, C. 2015. Become a successful leader of innovation and change. *Student Affairs Today* 18(6):12.

McGannon, H. (2012, March 1). Leadership is action, not position. *WordPress.* http://dx.doi.org/ https://aieseckpu.wordpress.com/2012/03/01/ leadership-is-action-not-position-donald-h-mcgannon/.

Mcintosh, M. A. 1998. *Mystical Theology.* Oxford: Blackwell.

Meyer, B. 2004. Christianity in Africa: from African independent to Pentecostal charismatic churches. *Annual Review of Anthropology* 33:447–474.

Moen, F., and E. Allgood. 2009. Coaching and the effect on self-efficacy. *Organization Development Journal* 274(4):69.

Moltmann, J. 1965. *Theologie der Hoffnung, Untersuchungen und Begründung und zu den Konsequenzen einer christlichen Eschatologie.* Munich: Chr. Kaiser Verlag.

Moore, B. V. 1927. The May conference on leadership. *Personnel Journal* 6:124–128.

Muluneh, G. S., and M. T. Gedifew. 2018. Leading changes through adaptive design: change management practice in one of the universities in a developing nation. *Journal of Organizational Change Management* 31(6):1249–1270. http://dx.doi.org/https://doi-org. ezproxy.regent.edu/10.1108/JOCM-10-2017-0379.

Mumford, M., and J. Van Doorn. 2001. The leadership of pragmatism: reconsidering Franklin in the age of charisma. *The Leadership Quarterly* 12:279–309.

Nanus, B. 1992. *Visionary Leadership: Creating a Compelling Sense of Direction for Your Organization.* San Francisco: Jossey-Bass Publishers.

Nelson, J. M. 2009. *Psychology, Religion, and Spirituality.* New York: Springer.

Newton, R. 2009. *The Practice and Theory of Project Management: Creating Value through Change.* Hampshire: Palgrave Macmillan.

Nonaka, I. 1988. Toward middle up-downward management: accelerating information creation. *Sloan Management Review* 9–18.

Nonaka, I. 1994. A dynamic theory of organizational knowledge creation. *Organization Science* 5:14–37.

Northouse, P. G. 2007. *Leadership: Theory and Practice.* 4th ed. Thousand Oaks: Sage.

Northouse, P. G. 2013. *Leadership: Theory and Practice.* 6th ed. Los Angeles: Sage.

Nutt, P. C. 1987. Identifying and appraising how manager installs strategy. *Strategy Management Journal* 8:1–14.

Okholm, D. 2009. Reformed ecclesiology: the community of Christ. *Presbyterians for Faith, Family and Ministry* 15(1):6.

Palmes, C. 1996. *Nueva espiritualidad de la vida religiosa en america latina.* Bogota: CLAR.

Parsloe, E., and M. Wray. 2001. *Coaching and Mentoring 2001.* Sterling: Kogan Page Publishers.

Peters, T. J., and R. H. Water Jr. 1982. *In Search of Excellence.* New York: Harper and Row.

Pettegree, A., and M. Hall. 2004. The reformation and the book: a reconsideration. *The Historical Journal* 47(4):785–808. http://dx.doi.org/http://dx.doi.org.ezproxy.regent.edu:2048/10.1017/S0018246X04003991.

Principe, W. 2000. *Toward Defining Spirituality in Exploring Christian Spirituality: An Ecumenical Reader* (edited by Kenneth J. Collins). Grand Rapids: Baker Books.

Prochaska, J. O., and C. C. DiClemente. 1982. Transtheoretical therapy: toward a more integrative model of change. *Psychotherapy: Theory, Research and Practice* 20:161–173.

Prochaska, J. O., and C. C. DiClemente. 1983. Stages and processes of self-change of smoking: toward an integrative model of change. *Journal of Consulting and Clinical Psychology* 51:390–395.

Prochaska, J. M., Prochaska, J. O., & Levesque, D. A. 2001. A transtheoretical approach to changing organizations. *Administration and Policy in Mental Health*, 28(4), 247-261.

Rahim, A., I. Civelek, and F. H. Liang. 2018. A process model of social intelligence and problem-solving style for conflict management. *International Journal of Conflict Management* 29(4):487–499. http://dx.doi.org/https://doi-org.ezproxy.regent.edu/10.1108/ IJCMA-06-2017-0055.

Rahner, K. 1975. "*World and Church,*" *Sacramentum Mundi.* New York: Seabury Press.

Randolph, S. A. 2013. Strategic thinking. *Workplace Health & Safety* 61(1):52. http://dx.doi.org/ http://dx.doi.org.ezproxy.regent. edu:2048/10.3928/21650799-20121221-56.

Richardson, L. 2009. *Sales Coaching: Making the Great Leap from Sales Manager to Sales Coach.* New York: McGraw-Hill.

Ridderbos, H. 1950. *De komst van het koninkrijk: Jezus' prediking volgens de synoptische evangeliën.* Kok: Kampen.

Robbins, J. 2004. The globalization of Pentecostal and charismatic Christianity. *Annual Review of Anthropology* 33:117–143.

Robert, D. 2000. Shifting southward: global Christianity since 1945. *International Bulletin of Missionary Research* 24:50–58.

Rokeach, M. 1973. *The Nature of Human Values.* New York: Free Press.

Rost, J. C. 1991. *Leadership for the Twenty-First Century.* New York: Prager.

Ruwhiu, D., and M. Cone. 2013. Pragmatic leadership: a return to wisdom. *Journal of Management and Organization* 19(1):25–43. http://dx.doi.org/http://dx.doi.org.ezproxy.regent.edu:2048/10.1017/jmo.2013.2.

Sarfraz, H. 2017. Strategic leadership development: simplified with Bloom's taxonomy, industrial and commercial training. *Industrial and Commercial Training* 49(1):40–47. http://dx.doi.org/https://doi-org.ezproxy.regent.edu/10.1108/ICT-08-2016-005.

Sarros, J. C., B. K. Cooper, and J. C. Santora. 2011. Leadership vision, organizational culture, and support for innovation in not-for-profit and for-profit organizations. *Leadership & Organization Development Journal* 32(3):291–309. http://dx.doi.org/http://dx.doi.org.ezproxy.regent.edu:2048/10.1108/01437731111123933.

Sashkin, M. 1988. "The Visionary Leader: A New Theory of Organizational Leadership." In *Charismatic Leadership: The Elusive Factor in Organizational Effectiveness*, edited by J. A. Conger and R. N. Kanungo. San Francisco: Jossey-Bass.

Sashkin, M. 1992. "Strategic Leadership Competencies: What Are They? How do They Operate? What Can Be Done to Develop Them?" In *Strategic Leadership: A Multiorganizational-Level Perspective*, edited by R. L. Phillips and J. G. Hunts. Westport: Quorum Books.

Sashkin, M., and R. M. Fulmer. 1988. *Toward an Organizational Leadership Theory,* edited by J. G. Hunt, B. R. Baliga, H. P. Dachler, and C. A. Schriesheim. Lexington: Emerging Leadership Vistas Books.

Sayles. 1993. *The Working Leader.* New York: The Free Press.

Schaefer, P. 2018. Why Small Business Fail: Top 7 Reasons for Startup Failure. https://www.businessknowhow.com/ startup/business-failure.htm.

Schein, E. H. 2010. Organizational Culture and Leadership. 4th ed. San Francisco: Jossey-Bass.

Schendel, D., and C. Hofer. 1979. *Strategic Management: A New View of Business Policy and Planning*. Boston: Little, Brown.

Schneider, W. E. 2000. Why good management ideas fail: the neglected power of organizational culture. *Strategy & Leadership* 28(1):24–29.

Schneiders, S. M. 1989. Spirituality in the academy. *Theological Studies* 50:676–697.

Scorgie, G. G., S. Chan, G. T. Smith, and J. D. Smith. 2011. *Dictionary of Christian Spirituality*. Grand Rapids: Zondervan.

Seeman, M. 1960. *Social Status and Leadership*. Columbus: Ohio State University, Bureau of Educational Research.

Sendjaya, S., and J. C. Sarros. 2002. Servant leadership: its origin, development, and application in organizations. *Journal of Leadership & Organizational Studies* 9(2):57–64.

Senge, P. M. 1990. *The Fifth Discipline: The Art and Practice of Learning Organization*. New York: Doubleday.

Schoemaker, P., S. Krupp, and S. Howland. 2013. Strategic leadership: the essential skills. *Harvard Business Review*, 131–136. http://dx.doi.org/https://hbr.org/2013/01/strategic-leadership-the-esssential-skills#.

Smircich, L. 1983. Concepts of culture and organizational analysis. *Administrative Science Quarterly* 28:339–358.

Smith, H. W. n.d. *The Christian's Secret of a Happy Life*. Old Tappan: Fleming H. Revell.

Sperry, L. 2003. Integrating spiritual direction functions in the practice of psychotherapy. *Journal of Psychology and Theology*, 31(1), 3-13.

Sporn, B. 2001. Building adaptive universities: emerging organizational forms based on experiences of European and us universities. *Tertiary Education and Management* 2(7):121–134.

Sternberg, R. J. 2002. "Successful Intelligence: A New Approach to Leadership." In *Multiple Intelligence and Leadership*, edited by R. E. Riggio, S. E. Murphy, and F. J. Pirozzolo, 9–28.

Stone, F. M. 2007. *Coaching, Counseling & Mentoring: How to Choose & Use the Right Technique to Boost Employee Performance.* http://dx. doi.org/https://ebookcentral-proquest-com.ezproxy.regent.edu.

Stonehouse, D. 2011. Management and leadership for support workers. *British Journal of Healthcare Assistants* 5(10):507–510.

Stonehouse, D. 2012. Resistance to change: the human dimension. *British Journal of Healthcare Assistants* 6(9):456–457.

Stonehouse, D. 2013. The change agent: the manager's role in change. *British Journal of Healthcare Management* 19(9):443–445. http://dx.doi.org/http://eres.regent.edu:2048/login?url=http://search.ebscohost.com/login.aspx?direct=true&db=ccm&AN=107972885&site=ehost-live.

Tanner, J., M. Ahearne, T. Leigh, C. Mason, and W. Moncrief. 2005. CRM in sales intensive organizations: A review and future directions. *Journal of Personal Selling and Sales Management* 25(2):170–180.

Taylor, C. M. 2007. *A Secular Age.* Cambridge: Belknap Press of Harvard University Press.

Taylor, C. M., C. J. Cornelius, and K. Colvin. 2014. Visionary leadership and its relationship to organizational effectiveness. *Leadership & Organization Development Journal* 35(6):566–583. http://dx.doi.org/ https://doi-org.ezproxy.regent.edu/10.1108/LODJ-10-2012-0130.

The Barna Group. 2002. Americans speak: Enron, WorldCom and others are result of inadequate moral training by families. https://www.barna.com/research/americans-speak-enron-world-com-and-others-are-result-of-inadequate-moral-training-by-families/.

Thomas, R. J., J. Belin, C. Jules, and N. Lynton. 2012. Global leadership teams: diagnosing three essential qualities. *Strategy & Leadership* 40(3):25–29. http://dx.doi.org/0-dx.doi.org.library.regent. edu/10.1108/10878571211221185.

Thompson, J. D. 1967. *Organization in Action: Social Science Bases of Administrative Theory.* New York: McGraw Hill.

Thorndike, R. L. 1920. Intelligence and its uses. *Harper's Magazine* 140:227–235.

Thornton, L. F. 2016. Understanding and Preventing Ethical Leadership Failures. https://leaderonomics.com/leadership/ ethical-leadership-failure.

Tomey, A. M. 2009. *Guide to Nursing Management and Leadership.* 8th ed. St. Louis: Mosby Elsevier.

Trice, H. M., and J. M. Beyer. 1993. *The Cultures of Work Organizations.* Englewood Cliffs: Prentice-Hall.

Tuck, K. n.d. Empowering the Next Generation Leaders. Retrieved March 19, 2019. https://strategicleaders.com/ empowering-next-generation-leaders/.

Van Maanen, J. 1979. "The Self, the Situation, and the Rules of Interpersonal Relations." In *Essays in Interpersonal Dynamics*, edited by W. Bennis, J. Van Maanen, E. J. Schein, and F. I. Steele, 43–101. Dorsey Press.

Van Maanen, J., and S. R. Barley. 1984. "Occupational Communities: Culture and Control in Organizations." In *Cummings, and Control, Research in Organizational Behavior,* edited by B. M. Staw and L. L. Cumming, 6. JAI Press.

Van Wyk, M. M. 2017. Exploring the role of the church as a "reformation agency" in enhancing a socially transformative agenda in South Africa. *Hervormde Teologiese Studies* 73(3). http://dx.doi.org/http://eres.regent.edu:2048/login?url=https://search-proquest-com.ezproxy.regent.edu/docview/1888701050?accountid=13479.

Vondey, W. 2008. *People of Bread: Rediscovering Ecclesiology.* New York: Paulist Press.

Vorster, M. 2015. Kingdom, church and civil society: a theological paradigm for civil action. *Hervormde Teologiese Studies* 71(3):1–7. http://dx.doi.org/http://eres.regent.edu:2048/login?url=https://search-proquest-com.ezproxy.regent.edu/docview/1738751600?accountid=13479.

Wainaina, N., K. Kabare, and E. Mukulu. 2014. Determinants of employee adaptability to transformational change in commercial in Nairobi, Kenya: empirical review. *International Journal of Academic Research in Business and Social Sciences* 10(4):1–9.

Waller, J. 2009. Getting serious about strategic influence. Center for Security Policy Occasional Paper. http://dx.doi.org/https://www.centerforsecuritypolicy. org/upload/wysiwyg/center%20publication %20pdfs/ Michael%20Waller%20-%20Getting%20Serious%20 About%20Strategic%20Influence.pdf.

Warren, R. 1995. *The Purpose Driven Church: Every Church Is Big in God's Eyes*. Michigan: Zondervan Press.

Weick, K. 1995. *Sensemaking in Organizations*. Thousand Oaks: Sage.

Weick, K., and K. M. Sutcliffe. 2001. *Managing the Unexpected*. San Francisco: Jossey-Bass.

Weisskopt, W.A. 1959. Existence and values. In A.H. Maslow (Ed.), new knowledge in human values. New York: Harper & Brothers.

Whelan-Berry, K. S., J. R. Gordon, and C. R. Hinings. 2003. Strengthening organizational change processes: recommendations and implications from a multilevel analysis. *The Journal of Applied Behavioral Science* 39(2):186–207. http://dx.doi.org/doi: 10.1177/0021886303256270.

Wicks, A., and R. E. Freeman. 1998. Organization studies and the new pragmatism: positivism, anti-positivism, and the search for ethics. *Organization Science* 9(2):123–140.

Wicks, R. J. 1995. *Handbook of Spirituality for Ministers*. New York: Paulist Press.

Willard, D. 2006. *The Great Omission: Reclaiming Jesus' Essential Teachings on Discipleship*. San Francisco: Harper Collins.

Williams, L. Q. 2017. How to Accept and Respect of Other Cultures. https://owlcation.com/social-sciences/ How-to-Accept-and-Respect-other-Cultures.

Winston, B. E., and K. Patterson. 2006. An integrative definition of leadership. *International Journal of Leadership Studies* 1(2):6–66.

Witherington, B. 2011. *Work: A Kingdom Perspective on Labor*. Grand Rapids: William B. Eerdmans Publishing Company.

Wright, N. T. 2010. *After You Believe: Why Christian Character Matters.* New York: Harper One.

Yukl, G. 1999. An evaluation of conceptual weaknesses in transformational and charismatic leadership theories. *Leadership Quarterly* 10(2):285–305.

Yukl, G., and R. Mashud. 2010. Why flexible and adaptive leadership is essential. *Consulting Psychology Journal: Practice and Research* 2(62):81–93.

Zhang, D., J. Zhao, L. Zhou, and J. Nunamaker Jr. 2004. Can e-learning replace classroom learning? *Communications of the ACM* 47(5):75–79.

Zhang, H., M. Cone, A. Everett, and A. Elkin. 2011. Aesthetic leadership in Chinese business: a philosophical perspective. *Journal of Business Ethics* 101:475–491.

Zhu, W., I. K. Chew, and W. D. Spangler. 2005. CEO transformational leadership and organizational outcomes: the mediating role of human-capital-enhancing human resource management. *The Leadership Quarterly* 16(1):39–52.